YOMIM NORAIM COMPANION

ROSH HASHANA
The Original Mother's Day

EIGHT MOTHERS OF THE DAY

WINNING THE COURT CASE
Ten Ideas to Merit Rachamim on the Yom HaDin

YOM KIPPUR INSPIRATION for KOL NIDREI and NEILAH

Rabbi Menachem Apter

Copyright © 2024

Published by:
Rabbi Menachem Apter
845-352-1561
rabbimapter@gmail.com

———————

Book & cover design by:

SRULY PERL | 845.694.7186
mechelp@gmail.com

לעלוי נשמת

אבי מורי
ר' צבי ב"ר מאיר נחום אפטר
נלב"ע ז' חשון תשס"א

אמי מורתי
יהודית בת יאיר
נלב"ע כ"א חשון תשפ"ד

מורי חמי
ר' קלונימוס משה ב"ר אלכסנדר אפרים עהרמאן
נלב"ע ז' כסלו תש"פ

חמותי
גיטל בת אלכסנדר
נלב"ע י"ג אייר תשפ"ג

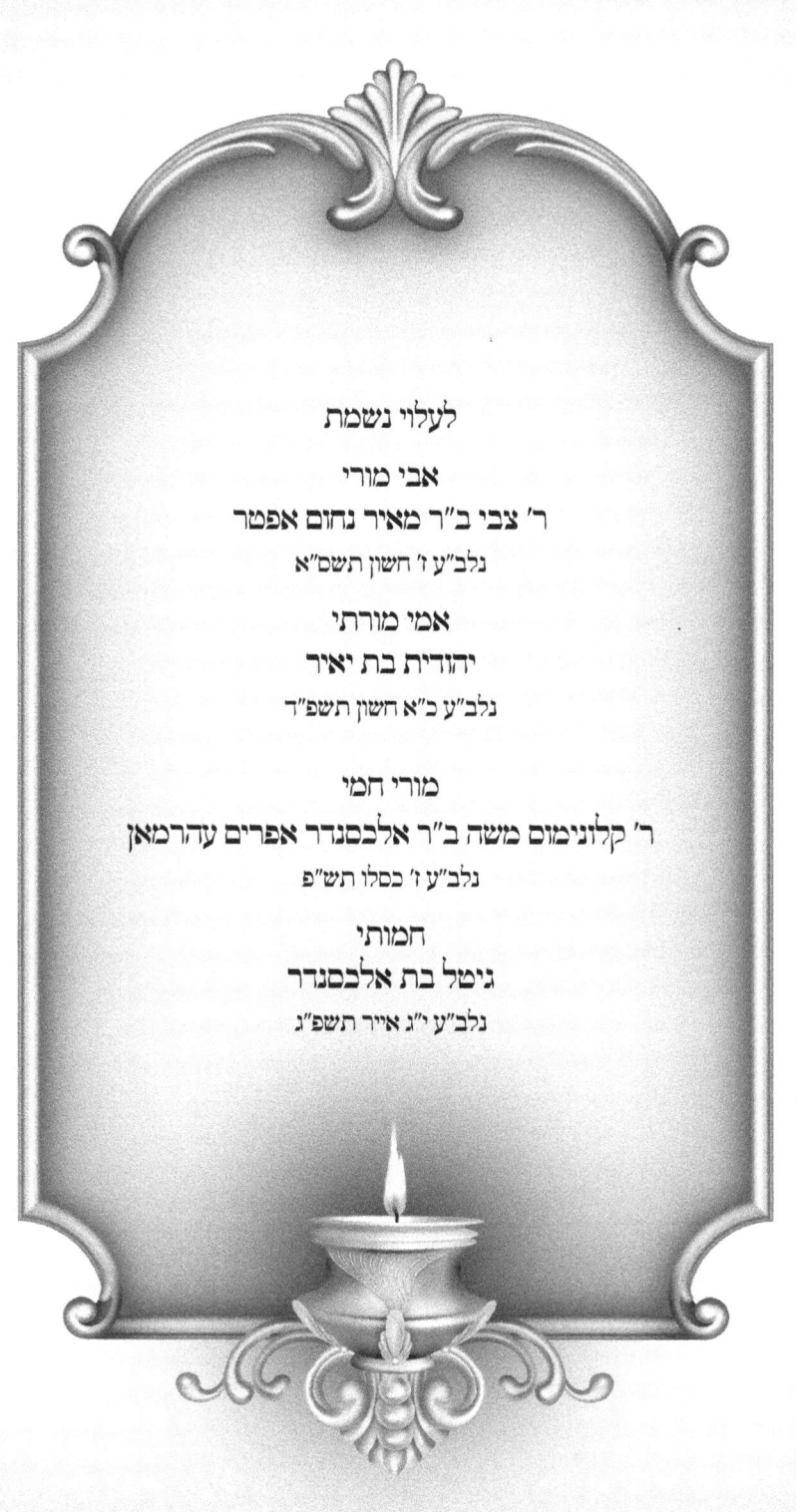

Table of Contents

Winning the Court Case

The Impending Court Case...9
Dan Lekaf Zechus...13
Zechus of the Tzibbur..17
Shana Sherasha Betchilasa..21
Ma'avir Al Midosav..27
Kol Hamerachem al Habrios...31
Simcha 37
Tefilla..41
Teshuva..47
The Thirteen *Middos* 53
Tzedaka..57
Summary of Ten Ideas to Win the "Court Case"..................61

Rosh Hashana: The Original Mother's Day

Rosh Hashana: The Original Mother's Day..........................67
Chava..71
Sarah...77
Hagar 83
The Mother of Sisra...89
Chana..95
Penina...103
Rivka...109
Rochel...113
Summary of Eight Mothers Related to Rosh Hashana.....119

Yom Kippur inspiration for Kol Nidrei and Neilah

Don't Be Like the Horses..123

Beware of the Satan..129

It's Not To Late..133

The Day that Lasts a Year..137

Step By Step...141

Act on the Inspiration..145

Take Action..149

Limud Zechus...151

Deep Down...155

Unconditional Love...159

Partial *Taharah*...161

A New "You"...165

Returning Home..169

You Can Do It..171

Embarrassed from *Cheit*..175

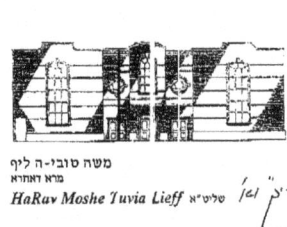

אגודת ישראל בית בנימין
Agudath Israel Bais Binyomin
2913-15 AVENUE L • BROOKLYN, N.Y. 11210

משה טובי-ה ליף
מרא דאתרא
HaRav Moshe Tuvia Lieff שליט"א

President
CHESKY PANETH

Executive Vice-Presidents
MARK KLEIN
MOSHE KOFMAN

Vice-President
MENDY JOSEFOVIC
MOSHE NUSSBAUM

Gabbaim
ITCHY BRAUN
YANKY SLAMOVITS

Treasurer
PINCHUS ZAGELBAUM

Secretary
BLIMIE SCHACHTER

Board of Directors
S"L HERSKOWITZ
ROBI HOFSTATTER
DAVID KATZ
DR. B.C. LIFSHITZ
BRUCE LISTHAUS
SHMAYA WEISNER

בס"ד

[handwritten Hebrew letter - text not clearly legible]

WINNING THE COURT CASE

Ten Ideas to Merit Rachamim on the Yom HaDin

The Impending Court Case

Rosh Hashana, the Yom Hadin, is approaching and a major court case is looming. Our very lives hang in the balance. We must prepare our defense without delay because time is running out. This trial which will decide the fate of our future is not taking place before a court of mortal beings; it is being conducted in front of the *Beis Din Shel Ma'alah*, the Heavenly Court.

The Rambam describes the days preceding Rosh Hashanah and Yom Kippur as days of *"pachad* and *mora."* [1] This theme is underscored in the moving prayer recited on Rosh Hashana and Yom Kippur, *Unesaneh Tokef.* In this *piyut*, we read *"umalachim yechafezun"*, that as the *Yemei Hadin* approach even the angels experience fear and trepidation. Also, one of the ten reasons that Rav Saadia Gaon gives for blowing the *shofar* on Rosh Hashana is to cause us to tremble and

---

1. *Perush HaMishnayos, Rosh Hashana* 4:7.

fear Hashem as the *Navi* Amos states, "Can a shofar be blown in the city and the people not tremble?"[2]

A famous story is told about Rabbi Aharon of Karlin, founder of the Karlin-Stolin chassidic dynasty. The story demonstrates the awe inspiring fear one should experience at this time of year. One Rosh Hashana morning, as the *Shaliach Tzibbur* began intoning the word "*HaMelech*," Rabbi Aharon fainted. When he revived, Rav Aharon said that upon hearing the declaration that *Hashem* is King, he was reminded of the following incident recorded in the *gemara*. The *gemara* relates that Rabban Yochanan ben Zakkai was smuggled out of the besieged city of Yerushalayim and came before the Roman general, Vespasian, to plead with him to spare the Torah center of Yavne. Rabban Yochanan began by addressing the general, "Peace be upon you, O king!" Vespasian responded, "You deserve to be executed, for if I am the king, why did you not come to me earlier?!"[3] Rav Aharon explained that he fainted because upon hearing the word "*HaMelech*" he envisioned *Hashem*, the King of the universe, sitting on His throne of judgment and declaring, "If I am King, why have you not come until now?!"

As Rosh Hashana arrives, we must recognize the significance of the impending court case and the possibilities of the judgment that awaits us. These should impel us to repent. Rav Chaim Friedlander notes that "fear is the source that brings to *teshuva*."[4] However, the purpose of fear is not to dishearten us or make us miserable. As Shlomo HaMelech writes, "Seven times does the *tzadik* fall and get up."[5] Rav Yitzchak Hutner explains that it is precisely through repeated falls that a person truly achieves righteousness. Struggles,

---

2. *Amos* 3:6.
3. *Gittin* 56a.
4. *Sifsei Chaim Moadim* 1 pg 50
5. *Mishlei* 24:16.

and even failures, are fundamental for the achievement of ultimate victory.

In the following pages, I am suggesting ten approaches and ideas, as taught by *Chazal,* to help win the "big court case". It is my fervent hope that the ideas presented in this booklet will propel you to make meaningful changes in your life and may *Hashem* bless you with a *shana tova umesuka.*

Dan Lekaf Zechus

Judging others favorably is a *mitzvas aseh* in the Torah, "*b'tzedek tishpot amisecha*" "Judge your fellow man with righteousness."[1] The *Gemara* suggests fulfilling this mitzvah as a fundamental way to merit a positive judgment: "One who judges his fellow man favorably will be judged favorably."[2] Since *Hashem* judges us in the manner that we judge others, if we are *dan lekaf zechus* in evaluating the actions of others, Hashem will be *dan lekaf zechus* in evaluating our deeds.

This equation is actually difficult to understand. We are mortal human beings who may very well lack full knowledge or understanding of the events that we see. Therefore, when we view a situation, we must draw our own conclusions. We have the choice to either judge harshly or kindly. *Hashem*, however, knows exactly what happened;

---

1. *Vayikra 19:15*
2. *Shabbos* 127b.

He doesn't have to make any assumptions. What, then, does it mean that He will judge us favorably? He has all the facts in front of Him!

When we say that *Hashem* will judge us *lekaf zechus*, we are not implying that He will invent possible explanations for our behavior or interpret our actions in a positive light, as we must do for others. Instead, we mean that He will mitigate his *middas hadin* with His *middas harachamim*. Although Hashem knows all the facts and is well aware of what we truly deserve, He will allow our individual circumstances and difficulties to soften our din when judging us.

Imagine that a man enters a subway car with his four young children. He sits down absentmindedly and pays no attention to the fact that his rambunctious children are disturbing the other passengers. After a few minutes, some angry passengers confront him. "Why don't you take care of your children? They are running all over the place and they're disturbing everyone!" The father jumps up and apologizes. "I am so sorry! I didn't realize all the trouble they are causing. We are on the way home from their mother's funeral and I am so distracted. I'll make sure to keep an eye on them from now on." Can you imagine the response from the other passengers? Suddenly, their anger is transformed into compassion. They just want to embrace these four young children and forget about all the trouble they caused. They were certainly not wrong in their original judgment; the children were misbehaving and deserved to be punished from the perspective of *middas hadin*. Once *middas harachamim* comes into the picture, however, the *din* is drastically transformed.

We all encounter similar situations in our daily lives. I recall a young student in my class who was consistently acting inappropriately and disturbing the whole class. Fortunately, before I punished him, I discovered that his home life was far from simple. His father had left home when he was a baby, and he was raised by his mother as an only child. His mother was now remarrying and his stepfather was about to move in with three daughters. It was no wonder that this young boy was acting out! Having this background information provided the *rachamim* that tempered my inclination towards *middas hadin*.

On Rosh Hashana, if we want *Hashem* to "judge us favorably" and take all our circumstances into account, we must do the same when judging others. As the Mishna in Pirkei Avos teaches us, "*Hevei dan es kol ha'adom lekaf zechus*" [3] The Mishna employs the term,"*kol ha'adom*" which literally means the whole man to teach us that the way to find merit in a fellow human being is to judge him as a whole, taking into account all his personal circumstances.

The Baal Shem Tov adds another dimension to the importance of judging others meritoriously. He teaches that every time we judge someone else, we are essentially passing judgment on ourselves and deciding our own punishment. We are given an opportunity to encounter a friend doing something similar to what we did. If we judge harshly and condemn our friend, we will not be able to defend ourselves against our own accusations. The same manner in which we judge our fellow man is the way we will be judged from Heaven.

This lesson is apparent from a famous story about Dovid HaMelech. Dovid sent Uria out to battle, and after Uria was killed at war, Dovid married Uria's widow, Basheva. In order to rebuke Dovid, Nosson HaNavi presented him with a "court case" to judge.[4] There were two neighbors, one rich and one poor; the wealthy man had many sheep and cattle, while the poor man had only one small lamb. When a guest came to visit the wealthy man, instead of taking an animal from his own livestock to prepare a meal, he took his destitute neighbor's lamb. Nosson asked Dovid what the appropriate judgment was in such a case. Dovid was incensed and quickly ruled that the wealthy man must pay back four times the value of the lamb to his poor neighbor. Upon hearing this, Nosson declared, "*Atah ha-ish*! You

---

3. *Avos 1:6*.

4. *Shmuel II 12*.

are the man!" In taking Basheva, Dovid had acted just as the wealthy man had. In issuing his ruling regarding the actions of the wealthy man, Dovid was actually judging himself. This is why, the Ralbag explains, four of Dovid's sons died during his lifetime – paralleling the price that Dovid said the wealthy man must pay. Had Dovid judged the wealthy man more favorably, perhaps he would not have been punished so severely.[5]

As the time of our judgment approaches and we focus on ensuring that *Hashem* will judge us with *rachamim*, we must turn our attention to this critical idea of being *dan lekaf zechus*. One of the best ways that we can guarantee for ourselves a good judgment this coming Rosh Hashana is if we commit to not being harsh in judging those around us, be they close family members, relatives, co-workers or friends. If we judge others leniently, *Hashem* will judge us the same way in return. May we all merit a favorable judgment!

---

5. For more on this idea, see Rav Yisroel Reisman's *Pathways of the Prophets*, p. 150.

Zechus of the Tzibbur

The *Gemara* provides two images of how *Hashem* judges us on Rosh Hashana. On the one hand, "*Kol ba'ei olam ovrin lefanav kivnei maron*"[1] – every individual passes before Him, just as each sheep passes under the staff of the shepherd. Each person is judged as an individual, on the basis of his own deeds. He is taken to task for any *lashon hara* he spoke, for any *bitul Torah* he caused, and for any lack of *kavana* in his *davening*. On the other hand, "*kulam niskorim biskira achas*" – All are marked with one marking.[2] This implies that we are judged as a unit, as part of mankind.

Hashem judges us individually and as a group. If a person does not survive the individual judgment, there is still hope for him when being judged as part of society. When judging the individual, *Hashem* takes

---

1. *Rosh Hashana* 16a.
2. *Rosh Hashana* 18a.

into account how many other people will be negatively impacted by this person's loss. How will others be affected by his lack of *parnassa* or good health? If he cannot afford to give *tzedaka* or is too unhealthy to volunteer his services, will others lose out as a result? Connecting to the tzibbur allows a person, who is undeserving of blessing, to be granted life only because of the other members of the klal who will struggle without his help. Thus, the more a person supports others and is involved in providing for the needs of the *tzibbur*, the greater are his chances for a good judgment on Rosh Hashana.

Rav Eliyahu Lopian writes that this is the meaning of the *pasuk*, "*Kel emuna ve'ein avel*," a G-d of trust with whom there is no wrongdoing.[3] Why do we praise *Hashem* by saying, "*ein avel*", He does no injustice? What kind of praise is this? If we were to praise a dignified individual, would it be fitting to say that he was "not bad"? Rav Lopian explains that "*ein avel*" means that *Hashem*'s decree is totally *emes*, as the *pasuk* states, "*Mishpitei Hashem emes, tzodku yachdav.*"[4] His judgments are truth because they are "all together righteous" – because they take all aspects into account. A human court cannot take into account the ramifications of its verdict. Human judges cannot let someone off the hook because his children will be orphans and his wife a widow. Even though their verdict is correct and just, there is an element of "*avel*" in it, as it negatively impacts some people who do not deserve to suffer. With *Hashem*'s judgment, in contrast, there is no wrongdoing – not for the judged one and not for anyone close who will be affected by the judgment of the individual – "*kulam niskorim beskira achas.*"

Rabbenu Bechayei explains that this is why we are prohibited to count the members of *Klal Yisroel* without the intermediary of the half-shekel.[5] When a person is counted as an individual, he is separated from the *klal*, and this is dangerous; when *Hashem* examines an

---

3. *Devarim* 32:4.
4. *Tehillim* 19:10.
5. *Shemos* 30:12.

individual's deeds on his own, he may be found unworthy of life. This idea is articulated by the Isha HaShunamis. When Elisha asked her if he should speak to the king on her behalf, she responded, "*Besoch ami anochi yoshaves*."[6] I would rather be part of the *klal* and not be singled out in case I am deserving of punishment.

The *Gemara* states that *Hashem* does not reject a *tefillas rabbim*.[7] When we *daven* along with others, our *tefillos* are more likely to be heard. However, our desire to be considered as part of the *tzibbur* is reflected in our personal *tefillos* as well, which are always phrased in the plural; when we *daven* for our personal needs, we include others as well. Similarly, we *daven* that *Hashem* heal an individual "*besoch sha'ar cholei Yisroel*" and that He comfort a mourner "*besoch sha'ar avlei Tziyon*." This is why, Tosfos suggests, we are permitted to begin our *Shmoneh Esrei* during the *Aseres Yemei Teshuva* with the request of "*Zachreinu LeChaim*," even though we ordinarily do not include personal requests in the first three *brachos*. It is forbidden to insert a personal request in these *brachos*; it is permitted to make a request for the *klal*.[8]

One who wants to merit a good judgment should make himself needed to the public. If we make sure that we are part of the *tzibur*, involved in providing for *Klal Yisroel*'s needs, and if we include *acheinu kol beis Yisroel* in our personal requests, we will merit to have all our *tefillos* answered.

---

6. *Melachim II* 4:13.

7. *Brachos* 8a.

8. Tosfos, *Brachos* 34A. Rav Mattisyahu Solomon (*Matnas Chaim, Yomim Nora'im*, p. 217) points out that Tosfos implies that if one thinks only of himself when he says "*Zachreinu LeChaim*," it would be considered a *hefsek* and his *tefilla* would not fulfill his obligation! During this time of year, if one does not include others in his *tefillos*, he cannot fulfill his obligation to *daven* at all!

Shana Sherasha Betchilasa

The *Gemara* suggests a rather strange *eitza* to help a person deserve a good year: "*Kol shana sherasha betchilasa misasheres besofa*," "Any year that begins poor will end rich."[1] Rashi explains that this has nothing to do with physical wealth or lack thereof. Rather, Yisrael is *zocheh* to a good year when they are "*osin atzman rashin beRosh Hashana*" – when they consider themselves poor on Rosh Hashana, and therefore turn to *Hashem* in prayer and supplication to fulfill their needs. If we realize at the beginning of the year that we are "poor" without *Hashem*'s help – that we have nothing without Him and that only He can provide what we need – then in the end, we will find that we are "rich," as He will generously provide for us.

Often, we manage to convince ourselves that we have no need for *Hashem*'s help. The story is told of a man who had an important

---

1. *Rosh Hashana* 16b.

business appointment that would likely lead to a deal worth millions of dollars. When he arrived, however, the parking lot was full, and he circled in vain looking for a spot. Glancing at the clock and feeling increasingly desperate, he started to pray. "*Hashem*, please help me find a parking spot! I will give ten thousand dollars to *tzedakah*!" Despite his heartfelt prayers, however, there was no spot to be found, and it was getting later and later. He tried again. "I will *daven* with a *minyan* every day!" But there was still no parking spot, and he would soon miss the appointment entirely. In a final desperate attempt, he pleaded, "I will start learning *Daf Yomi*! Just please help me!" At that moment, a car pulled out of a spot right at the entrance of the building and the man quickly parked his car and ran inside. As he ran to make his appointment, he looked up to heaven and said, "Thanks anyway, but I found one on my own!" Even when we ask *Hashem* for help and He provides for us, we imagine that we don't really need Him after all.

We generally feel in need of *Hashem*'s help when life is complicated or difficult. When we're negotiating a major business deal or need a significant *yeshua*, we realize that we can accomplish nothing without Him. Indeed, we often take our bank accounts, our health, and our relationships for granted; we *daven* only when we feel that we are not managing on our own. The truth is, however, that we are always dependent on *Hashem*, even for the little things in life and even to maintain what we already have. Just because you have a job, a family, and good health today does not mean it will stay that way. When we feel that we are "poor," that everything we have or could have depends on *Hashem*, we automatically turn to Him to provide for us.

Sometimes, it takes a jolt to make us realize just how much we are dependent on *Hashem*. When Yaakov was fleeing to Charan, *Hashem* appeared to him in a dream and promised him, "Your offspring shall be as the dust of the earth, and you shall spread out powerfully westward, eastward, northward, and southward..."[2] On the simple level, this is a *bracha* that Yaakov's children will be as numerous as the dust. The Kli Yakar explains the *pasuk* differently, however. He writes that when *Klal Yisrael* hit rock bottom, when they are as lowly as the dust of the earth, that is precisely when their salvation will come. Until they reach that point of desperation, *Klal Yisrael* won't turn to *Hashem* for help; they will convince themselves that they can find their own way out of their difficulties. Only when they recognize that all of their attempts are futile and that they need *Hashem*'s help will He respond to their pleas.

This message was driven home to me when my community was hit by Hurricane Sandy in October 2012. Entire neighborhoods were wiped out, and many areas resembled war zones. Over a million people – including myself and my neighbors – lost electricity for well over a week. It was dark, cold, and very humbling. The common refrain wherever I turned was, "I have no power!" From a practical perspective, this aptly describes the situation; there was no electricity in the entire region. But this statement is also very profound. When the things we take for granted are suddenly taken away from us, we are forced to concede that we essentially have no power. The only one we can turn to for help is *Hashem*.

Yosef HaTzaddik excelled at this *midda*. Under all circumstances, he recognized that *Hashem* provides everything. After spending years in jail, Yosef was finally given the opportunity to be free. But when Pharaoh said to him, "I heard it said of you that you comprehend a dream to interpret it,"[3] Yosef's response was, "*Biladai*! That is beyond me; it is G-d who will respond."[4] Pharaoh did not believe in *Hashem*; Yosef was taking a risk that he would be sent straight back to jail. Yosef, however, would under no circumstances deny the truth – that

---

2. *Breishis* 28:14.
3. *Breishis* 41:15.
4. *Breishis* 41:16.

Hashem, and not he, is in control. He acknowledged that everything is in the hands of *Hashem*.

The *Sfas Emes* notes that we reiterate that everything is from *Hashem* every day in our *davening* when we recite *Mizmor LeSoda*: "Know that *Hashem* is G-d; He created us, *velo anachnu*."[5] The word "*velo*" is a *kri uksiv*. It is written with a *vav*, so that the *pasuk* means, "He created us, and we are His." It is read, however, with an *alef*, so that the *pasuk* means, "He created us, and not us." Part of our expression of gratitude to *Hashem* is recognition that we cannot accomplish anything on our own, that "my strength and the power of my hand"[6] can do nothing without *Hashem*'s help. When one reaches the level of recognizing that all is from *Hashem*, then "*lo*" with an *alef* becomes "*lo*" with a *vav* – we become closer to *Hashem*; we "belong" to Him. Similarly, the *Sfas Emes* explains, the word *Elul* is made up of the letters of "*lo*" with an *alef* and "*lo*" with a *vav*. The *avoda* of Elul is to understand that "*velo anachnu*," that we can accomplish nothing on our own, so that we can reach the level of "*velo anachnu*," belonging to *Hashem*.[7]

On Rosh Hashana, everything is at stake. This is our opportunity to beg for our lives and to ask for everything that we need, but we can only be successful if we begin the year "poor," recognizing that only *Hashem* can provide our needs. This is, in fact, the central theme of Rosh Hashana, when we accept *Hashem*'s *malchus* upon ourselves. When we declare, "*Umalchuso bechol mashala*," we acknowledge that *Hashem* rules over every aspect of our lives. If we begin the year by

---

5. *Tehillim* 100:3.

6. *Devarim* 8:17.

7. The Chasam Sofer makes a similar point in his interpretation of Yaakov's statement upon waking from his dream: "Surely *Hashem* is present in this place, *va'anochi lo yadati*, and I did not know" (*Breishis* 28:16). The Chasam Sofer writes that when one can declare, "*Va'anochi lo yadati*," "I do not recognize the I," *Hashem* is surely in that place. *Hashem* can be found when one does not focus on himself.

internalizing this, we will end the year "rich," with all of our *tefillos* answered.

Ma'avir Al Midosav

Chazal tell us that "*Kol hama'avir al midosav, ma'avirin lo al kol pesha'av.*"[1] On the simple level, this means that if someone wrongs you and you overlook that wrongdoing, you will be treated in a similar manner by *Hashem*. *Midda keneged midda*, measure for measure, *Hashem* will similarly ignore your transgressions when it comes time to judge you for your sins.

The *Gemara* relates that Rabbi Akiva excelled at this particular trait.[2] Following an extended period of drought, Rabbi Eliezer recited twenty-four requests for rain, but none was forthcoming. When Rabbi Akiva recited *Avinu Malkeinu*, however, it immediately began to rain.

---

1. *Rosh Hashana* 17a.
2. *Ta'anis* 25b.

Seeing this, the people began to question Rabbi Eliezer's piety. A *bas kol* emanated from Heaven and declared that Rabbi Akiva was, in fact, no greater than Rabbi Eliezer; the only reason that Rabbi Akiva was answered was that he was *"ma'avir al midosav."*

Rav Yisroel Salanter notes that if Rabbi Akiva was *ma'avir al midosav* and Rabbi Eliezer was not, it would seem to imply that Rabbi Akiva was indeed greater. What, then, did the *bas kol* mean in distinguishing between the two great rabbis in this way?

Rav Salanter explains that there was a general dispute between Rabbi Eliezer and Rabbi Akiva regarding the proper manner in which one should conduct himself. Rabbi Akiva emphasized the importance of *middas harachamim*, the trait of mercy, while Rabbi Eliezer chose the path of *middas ha'emes* and *middas hadin*, the trait of truth and justice. In this, they followed in the footsteps of their teachers, Hillel and Shammai.[3] The path of Rabbi Eliezer was not inferior or less righteous in any way than the path of Rabbi Akiva, but his choice had certain consequences. When Rabbi Eliezer, the man of *middas hadin*, prayed for rain, *Hashem* responded to him in kind – with *middas hadin*. *Klal Yisroel* were not worthy of rain according to the strict parameters of justice, so Rabbi Eliezer's *tefilla* was not answered. Rabbi Akiva, however, was a man of *middas harachamim*; he was *"ma'avir al midosav."* As a result, when he prayed for rain, *Hashem*

---

3. The *gemara* (*Shabbos* 30b) relates the famous story of the prospective convert who wished to learn the entire Torah while standing on one foot. Shammai chased him away, while Hillel took the time to educate him. This does not reflect, as commonly thought, that Hillel was a compassionate person and Shammai was mean-spirited. Both Hillel and Shammai had exemplary character traits; they simply disagreed regarding the proper general guidelines for behavior. Shammai *paskened* in accordance with *middas hadin*. He felt that the man lacked respect for the Torah, and he was therefore halachically required to send him away. Hillel, in contrast, *paskened* in accordance with *middas harachamim*; he felt that one is permitted to be lenient and bend the rules in order to draw a person closer to Torah. Similarly, Hillel rules that we tell every bride, *"Kallah na'eh ve-chasuda,"* whether she is beautiful or not, as every bride is beautiful in the eyes of her husband. Shammai, however, maintains that we cannot bend the truth; we cannot tell a bride that she is beautiful if this is not objectively true.

responded to him in kind – with mercy. Even though *Klal Yisroel* did not deserve the rain, *Hashem* answered Rabbi Akiva's plea.

If we want *Hashem* to respond to our *tefillos* with *rachamim*, ignoring our shortcomings to provide us with what we desire, we must act accordingly. When someone angers or upsets us, we must look the other way and be forgiving – and then *Hashem* will act the same way with us. If your father, mother-in-law, spouse, child, boss, or coworker insults you and you do not respond or harbor resentment towards them, *Hashem* will similarly forgive your *aveiros*.

I heard a beautiful story that illustrates the power of this *midda*. There was a young boy who was not exceptionally smart, and it took him a long time to catch on to things. Everyone would get frustrated with him, and his classmates often mistreated him. Despite their taunts, this boy had an exceptional character, and he did not respond; he remained silent. At some point, however, the boy's father noticed that whenever the boy was insulted, he would mumble under his breath. The father was concerned. It seemed that the boy could no longer take the abuse.

When he asked his son what had changed, the boy explained that he had read a story about a couple who did not have children for many years. Rav Chaim Kanievsky advised them to receive a *bracha* from someone who fulfills the qualifications of *"ne'elavim ve'einam olvim,"* someone who does not respond when insulted. After some time, they found such a person and received the desired *bracha* – and nine months later, they were blessed with a child. When he read this story, the boy explained, he realized that he had a tremendous *ko'ach*. Since he never responded to the many insults he received, his *brachos* would surely be fulfilled! Since no one asked him for a *bracha*, he decided to take action. Whenever he heard the name of a sick person, he would memorize it. And whenever someone insulted him, he would mumble those names under his breath, *davening* for their *refua*!

The *gemara* states that the world stands in the *zechus* of those who keep quiet during an argument and do not respond.[4] If someone offends you and you are certain that you are in the right, but you nevertheless control yourself and do not respond, you have acquired the merit of sustaining the entire world! Such an act will certainly serve you well when you stand before the Heavenly Court on *Yom HaDin*. Someone who saves even one life has a special *zechus* in his corner when he is judged – all the more so someone who is responsible for saving the world!

---

4. *Chullin* 89a.

Kol Hamerachem al Habrios

The Torah commands that an *ir hanidachas*, a city in which the majority of the inhabitants worship *avoda zara*, must be entirely wiped out. If we fulfill this command, the *pasuk* promises, "*Ve-nasan lecha rachamim ve-richamcha*"[1] – Hashem will grant you the ability to have *rachamim*, and then He will have compassion on you. *Chazal* learn from here that "*Kol hamerachem al habrios, merachamin alav min hashamayim*," "Whoever has mercy on others, *Hashem* will have mercy on him from Heaven."[2] The Ba'al Shem Tov explains that *Hashem*'s behavior towards us mirrors our own behavior. This is the meaning of the phrase, "*Hashem tzilcha*," "*Hashem* is your protective shade."[3] Just as one's shadow replicates his every move, *Hashem*'s actions reflect our own. Therefore, we have the ability

---

1. *Devarim* 13:18.
2. *Shabbos* 151b.
3. *Tehillim* 121:5.

to arouse the *midda* of *rachamim* in *HaKadosh Baruch Hu* by treating others with *rachmanus*.

The Ohr HaChaim explains that this is precisely why the pasuk states, "*Ve-nasan lecha rachamim*" immediately after we wipe out the *ir hanidachas*. In order to properly fulfill the *mitzva*, one must act cruelly, and this will certainly affect one's personality. Killing others, even if justified, turns the executioner into a cruel individual, a person who is incapable of mercy. If one were to remain in such a state, one would not deserve *Hashem*'s compassion, as Hakodosh Baruch Hu deals with us *midda kenegged midda*. That being the case, no one would be willing to fulfill the *mitzva* of destroying an *ir hanidachas*. Therefore, *Hashem* promises us that anyone who fulfills this commandment will be granted the attribute of compassion, despite his outwardly cruel act, and as a result, "*ve-richamcha*," Hashem will have mercy on him as well.[4]

This idea is emphasized in a Chassidic interpretation of the *pasuk*, "Yitzchak loved Esav *ki tzayid befiv*."[5] Is it possible that Yitzchak Avinu loved his wayward son simply because he provided him with good food? Reb Meir of Premishlan explained this *pasuk* based on a story about his *rebbe*, the Be'er Mayim Chaim. The Be'er Mayim Chaim had a difficult son who did not follow in his footsteps and caused him great anguish. Despite all the difficulties in raising this son, however, he loved him and showed great care for him. He was once overheard *davening*, "I have so much pain from my son, yet I still do everything possible for him. Likewise, *Hashem*, even if Your children, *Klal Yisrael*, cause you pain, ignore the pain and take care of them!" The Gemora tell us that in the future Yitzchok will use a similar argument in

---

4. Rav Moshe Feinstein derives a *halacha* from this statement of the Ohr HaChaim (*Igros Moshe C*hoshen Mishpat 2:47). Since killing is an act of cruelty that automatically affects the killer, when a person must kill a fly or mosquito that is bothering him, he should at least make an effort to avoid killing the bug directly with his hands. If one must be that compassionate on a bug, how much more so with people!

5. *Breishis* 25:28.

defense of *Klal Yisroel*. Hashem will complain to the *Avos* that their children, *Klal Yisroel*, have sinned and Avrohom and Yaakov will respond, "Let them be annihilated for the sake of your Holy name." Yitzchok will be the only one who will plead on their behalf with the following: "Though they have sinned, they deserve your love, because they are your children." Yitzchok will prove his case by stating that he, too, had a son who sinned and yet he loved him merely because he was his son. Thus, Reb Meir of Premishlan explains, Yitzchak loved Esav "*ki tzayid befiv*", through him he had "food for argument" with which to defend Klal Yisroel and assure their survival.[6]

This type of merciful judgment is what Yaakov Avinu was hoping for when he sent Binyamin to Mitzrayim along with his other sons. Before sending them off, he gave them a *bracha*: "May *Hashem* grant you mercy before the man (*lifnei ha'ish*), that he may release to you your other brother as well as Binyamin."[7] Although in context, the word "*lifnei*" means "before" physically, in front of the man, the Taz interprets it to mean "before" earlier, in time.[8] Yaakov's *bracha* to his sons was that *Hashem* should grant them an opportunity to act with compassion *lifnei ha'ish*, before they arrived at the palace of the viceroy of Egypt. Then, since they acted with mercy on others, the man would have mercy on them. When one wants mercy from a king, the best way to attain it is by acting with compassion beforehand.

It is natural that someone in a position of authority will judge those who are kind to others with kindness. I experienced this myself when I taught an elementary school class in which one student was severely handicapped. While all of his classmates treated him well and included him in their games, one particular boy did more than the others. He walked with him to recess every day, helped him when he needed something, encouraged him, and was very patient with

---

6. See *Shabbos* 89b.
7. *Breishis* 43:14.
8. Taz, *Orach Chaim* 5850.

him. I respected this boy and felt special warmth towards him. In fact, if he misbehaved in any way, I would always try to look the other way. *HaKodosh Baruch Hu* similarly reciprocates with kindness when He sees us dealing with others kindly.

We don't always see how this equation plays out in real life, but I heard a story in which the connection between one person's benevolence and *Hashem*'s kindness in return is very clear. There was a man in Montreal who used to park his car near his *shul* every Erev Shabbos so that it would be available immediately after Shabbos. A Hatzolah volunteer in the *shul* asked if the man would mind giving him a set of car keys just in case there was an emergency call in the middle of Shabbos and the car would prove helpful. After considering the idea, the man agreed and gave the volunteer a set of keys. One Shabbos, the volunteer received a call on his Hatzolah radio. He quickly jumped into the man's car and proceeded to the designated address. Witnessing this, the car owner was happy to have had the privilege of helping to save a life. After davening, he returned home – only to find that the life he had helped save was that of his daughter. The baby had swallowed a large bead that had become stuck in her throat, and she had turned blue. His wife immediately called Hatzolah, and the volunteer – who arrived in the girl's father's car – managed to release the bead as the child was gasping for breath. The Hatzolah volunteer told the father that were it not for the vehicle at his disposal when he received the call, the young girl would have suffered severe damage. He demonstrated caring and compassion by loaning his car and *Hashem* reciprocated with compassion by saving his daughter's life.

We are unfortunately surrounded by *tzaros* and inundated with opportunities to have *rachmanus* on others. We can help by donating money to a poor family or giving time to someone in need. We can get involved in organizations such as Hatzolah, Tomchei Shabbos, Chaverim, or Chai Lifeline. Even if we don't have the money or the time, we can always give *chizuk* and empathy to people who are suffering –

a widow, a divorcee, an orphan, or an older single. Even just a smile or a warm word can make a tremendous difference in someone else's life. If we cultivate this trait of compassion in ourselves, then even if we are undeserving, *Hashem* will treat us in kind and hear our plea, "*Shema Koleinu Chus V'rachem Aleinu*".

Simcha

The period of Rosh Hashana and Yom Kippur is termed the *"Yamim Nora'im,"* literally, "The Days of Awe." This is a time of great fear, as we prepare ourselves for the upcoming judgment. Indeed, on the first night of *Slichos*, we declare, *"Zochalin veoradin miyom bo'acha,"* "We are trembling and quaking from the day You will come." In each *Amida* that we recite on Rosh Hashana and Yom Kippur, we ask that *HaKadosh Baruch Hu* grant us the ability to fear Him properly – *"Vechein tein pachdecha."*

Nevertheless, when Rav Avigdor Miller was asked what the central *avoda* of Rosh Hashana is, he responded that it is to be *besimcha*, to be happy! How can we understand this, given the overwhelming atmosphere of fear and trembling that envelopes this period?

The Rambam describes how each individual should view himself standing before the Heavenly court, with the merits and demerits of the entire world evenly balanced on the scales before him. Even one *mitzva* that he does has the ability to tip the world *likaf zechus*, to the side of merit, and therefore salvation, and each *aveira* that he does has the ability to tip the judgment of the world in the other direction.[1] How can we be sure that our *mitzvos* will have the necessary impact?

The *Orchos Tzaddikim* writes: "When one performs a *mitzva* with joy, his reward is a thousand times greater than that of one who performs the *mitzva* as though it is a burden."[2] Rabbeinu Ovadia MiBartenura similarly writes that when a person does a *mitzva* with *simcha*, the *simcha* itself is counted as a *mitzva*; every *mitzva* performed with *simcha* counts as a double *mitzva*.[3] The *Sefer Chareidim* also writes that the "primary reward for a *mitzva* is for the great joy one has in performing it."[4] Performing *mitzvos* with *simcha* increases their "weight," which surely helps tip the scales.

Why does doing *mitzvos* with *simcha* have such an important effect? We can understand this by way of a *mashal*. Reuven and Shimon work for the same company and perform the same work. Reuven is a diligent worker who always comes on time and works diligently throughout the day, while Shimon is always a bit tardy and wastes a lot of time. One day, the boss moves Shimon to a corner office with a private secretary and gives him a significant raise. Reuven is incensed and confronts his boss. Why does this treatment make any sense? The boss explains that while it is true that Shimon is not a great worker, he came up with an idea that helped the company grow and increased profitability. Small indiscretions are insignificant compared to the success that he brings to the whole company, and he therefore deserves to be rewarded.

---

1. *Hilchos Teshuva* 3:4.
2. *Orchos Tzaddikim, Shaar Hasimcha*
3. *Avos* 4:2
4. *Sefer Chareidim*

Similarly, when a person does *mitzvos* with *simcha*, others see his enthusiasm, excitement, and passion, and they want to be "part of the company;" they imitate him and do *mitzvos*. Because he "helps the company grow," his mistakes are overlooked and his *mitzvos* carry more weight.[5]

Why is encouraging others to do *mitzvos* so important? The entire purpose of this world is to increase *kavod shamayim*. *Chazal* teach us, "All that *HaKadosh Baruch Hu* created in His world, He created solely for His glory."[6] Similarly, we declare in one of the *sheva brachos*, "*Shehakol bara lichvodo*," "He created everything for His honor." The *Sfas Emes* notes that we also say, "*Baruch Elokeinu sheberaánu lichvodo*," blessing *Hashem* for creating *Klal Yisrael* specifically to give Him honor. While everything was created for *kavod shamayim*, we, the *Am Hanivchar*, were created to reveal the *kavod shamayim* to the world. What better way to accomplish this than by demonstrating that we feel fortunate and happy to be *ovdei Hashem*!

---

5. The *Chovos HaLevovos* writes (*Sha'ar Ahavas Hashem*) that even a person on a very high spiritual level does not attain the level of one who encourages others to follow the right path, as doing so multiplies his *zechuyos* every moment. If other people are influenced by the way he performs a *mitzva*, he receives credit for all of the *mitzvos* done because of him.

The opposite is also true. The *Gemara* tells us (*Brachos* 35b) that if someone benefits from this world without reciting a *bracha*, it is considered as though he stole from *Hashem*. Indeed, the *Gemara* says, such a person is comparable to Yeravam ben Nevat. Rashi explains that just as Yerovom caused the Jewish People to worship idols, a person who eats without a *bracha* causes others to sin when they watch him and copy his actions. This is true even though Yeravam deliberately enticed the people to sin, while one who eats without a *bracha* has no intention of encouraging others to follow his example. Every person is responsible for the consequences of his actions; if others learn from him, he is held accountable. The *Beis HaLevi* explains that this is the meaning of the *mishna*'s statement, "*Nifra'in min ha'adam mida'ato veshelo mida'ato*" (*Pirkei Avos* 3:16). We are also punished for sins that we have no idea we did – as when others learned from our *aveiros*. If this is the effect of passively influencing others to do the wrong thing, imagine the effect of passively causing someone to do a *mitzva*! *Chazal* tell us that the value of a good deed is five hundred times that of doing something evil.

6. *Pirkei Avos* 6:11.

It is thus not surprising that Rav Miller said that the *avoda* of Rosh Hashana is to be *besimcha*. Through *simcha*, we can fulfill our mission in this world – "*shebera'anu lichvodo.*"

Tefilla

On Rosh Hashana and Yom Kippur, we repeatedly declare, "*Uteshuva utefilla utzedaka ma'avirin es ro'a hagezeira.*" One of the methods of assuring success in our judgment is prayer. The *gemara* elaborates that crying out to *Hashem* is one of the ways that we can wipe out an evil decree.[1]

Not all prayers are equal, however. The *Gemara* recounts the story of two individuals who were ill. One *davened* and recovered from his sickness, while the other *davened* and did not recover. The *Gemara* explains that the first man *davened* a "*tefilla shleima,*" whereas the other did not. Rashi explains that a *tefilla shleima* is a *tefilla* said with *kavana*. Only this type of *tefilla* is answered by *Hashem*. But how is it possible that the second man lacked *kavana* in his *tefilla* when his life was at stake? It would seem that *kavana* does not only refer to

---

1. *Rosh Hashana* 16b.

appropriate focus and concentration, which the second man surely had. Rather, it refers to the recognition that everything comes from *Hashem* and that we are completely dependent on him.

The story is told of a person who approached the Chazon Ish for a *bracha* just before *Kol Nidrei*. The Chazon Ish asked him, "Do you have a *parnassa*?" The man responded, "The last thing I'm thinking about right now, on Erev Yom Kippur, is *parnassa*!" The Chazon Ish replied, "The only reason you are not thinking about *parnassa* is that you think that you can take care of it yourself. If you really believed that you are totally dependent on *Hashem* for everything, even for the bread on your table, you would certainly be concerned about *parnassa* on Erev Yom Kippur!"

Once we recognize and accept that everything is from *Hashem*, the next step is to realize that *Hashem* is *kol yachol* and can accomplish anything. This is the premise of a *tefilla shleima* – nothing is too difficult for *Hashem*. Some people *daven* for a *choleh* while the phone number of the *chevra kadisha* is in their back pocket. Can that be considered a *tefilla shleima*? Our *tefillos* must reflect our *emuna* that *HaKadosh Baruch Hu* can do anything – even save someone for whom the doctors have given up all hope.

When we say that *Hashem* is "*kol yachol*," we mean that He even has the ability to put an elephant through the eye of a needle. Obviously, He can shrink the elephant or expand the needle – but He can even get the elephant through the eye of the needle without changing a thing. He can do things that seem absolutely impossible to the human mind. Yet, nothing is impossible for *Hashem*.

The *Shulchan Aruch* provides us with another method of ensuring that our *tefillos* are accepted: "One who recites the following four phrases will be *zocheh* to greet the *Shechina*: *Asei lema'an shemecha, asei lema'an yeminecha, asei lema'an Torasecha, asei lema'an kedushasecha.*"[2] This *halacha* seems to provide a magic formula, but we all say these words at the end of our *Shmoneh Esrei* every day, and our *tefillos* are not always answered. Obviously, merely saying the words is not enough; we must genuinely intend their meaning. The way to have our prayers answered is to focus not on the fulfillment of our own needs, but on the ultimate goal – *lema'an shemecha, lema'an yeminecha*. We must not be *mispallel* for our personal benefit, but rather with the goal of improving our *avodas Hashem*. If we are healthy, have few worries about *parnassa*, and have *menuchas hanefesh*, we will be able to serve *Hashem* better. If this is truly our *kavana* when we say these words, our *tefillos* will be accepted.

I heard a *mashal* that illustrates this point. A wealthy man who owned a construction supply store raised an orphan from childhood and trained the boy in the construction business. Eventually, this boy became very successful and wealthy. One day, the young man approached his benefactor and said, "Everything I have today I owe to you. I would like to do something special for you. Your house is old and needs renovation, and I would like to build you a new beautiful and modern house." His adoptive father accepted the gift on the condition that all of the materials for the house would be taken from his supply store.

Every day, the construction workers would pick up the day's supply of materials from the warehouse. When they arrived, there was a long line of people waiting, but they were escorted to the front of the line, where they took their materials and left without paying. The other workers wondered why these men were given special treatment, but when they heard that they were building for the owner of the store, everything became clear to them.

HaKadosh Baruch Hu similarly has a "store" full of *nachas, gezunt, parnassa*, and *bracha*. If we use these "supplies" to build for Him, then

---

2. *Orach Chaim* 122:3.

He will give us all our needs up front, at no cost. We stress this in all of our *tefillos* during the period of the *Yomim Nora'im* when we request, "*Zochreinu lechaim... lema'ancha Elokim chaim.*" We request life not for ourselves, but *lema'ancha*, for *Hashem*'s sake – so that we can best serve Him.

A friend of mine suffered from hip and knee problems for many years. Although he tried numerous remedies and surgeries, nothing worked; he still had difficulty bending and would often fall. He then heard about a new type of surgery that would improve his situation if successful, but it was a risky operation. He decided to consult with Rav Chaim Kanievsky and ask him if he should undergo the surgery. He began to explain the procedure involved, but Rav Chaim did not want to hear the details. The only question he asked was whether my friend, in his present condition, was able to bow for *korim* on Yom Kippur. My friend replied that he could not. Rav Chaim then asked if he would be able to bow for *korim* if the surgery was successful, and my friend said that he would. Rav Chaim told him to have the surgery and that it would *im yirtza Hashem* be successful.

When my friend relayed this story to me, I couldn't understand what Rav Chaim was getting at. Why did he feel that the fulfillment of *korim* was so important? It is only a *minhag*, not a *chiyuv*, and there are many people who are unable to do it due to their physical limitations. After giving the matter some thought, I realized that Rav Chaim was simply trying to find a reason to have the operation *l'shem shamayim*, for *Hashem*'s sake. If that was the goal, he knew that the surgery would be successful.

Chazal tell us that while the gates of *tefilla* are sometimes closed, they are always open during the *Aseres Yemei Teshuva*.[3] We have a special opportunity that should not be wasted. We must use this time properly to recognize our dependence on *Hashem* and to *daven* for

---

3. *Brachos* 32.

our needs and those of *Klal Yisrael* so that we can all serve *Hashem* better. In that merit, our *tefillos* will be answered!

Teshuva

Chazal advise every person to do *teshuva* one day before his death.[1] Obviously, none of us know precisely when that day will be, leaving us with no choice but to repent every single day. Each day is an opportunity to consider how close we are to fulfilling our mission in this world – or how far we are from that goal – and a chance to reorient ourselves to the right course. I often think of this when I visit my family in England, as acquaintances predictably ask, "Why are you here and how long will you be staying?" These are actually profound questions that each one of us should consider every day of our lives. Why am I here? What is my purpose and mission? And how long do I really think I have to accomplish it? These questions should be an impetus for daily *teshuva*.

---

1. *Avos* 2:10.

Although every day is an opportunity for *teshuva*, the Rambam writes that *teshuva* is especially appropriate during the *Aseres Yemei Teshuva*, when *Hashem* is more open to accepting our repentance. [2] Moreover, *teshuva* is one of the three methods through which we can avert the evil decree during the *Yomim Nora'im* – "*Uteshuva utefilla utzedaka ma'avirin es ro'a hagezeira.*"[3]

There are a number of impediments to proper *teshuva*. The first step in the *teshuva* process is admission of guilt. This is not as simple as it sounds, however, as people naturally tend to justify their actions. In fact, after the very first sin in human history, Adam HaRishon immediately blamed his wife.[4] In contrast, when Nosson HaNavi confronted Dovid HaMelech after his sin with Basheva, he responded "*Chatasi,*" "I have sinned."[5] The Sforno comments that whereas Dovid was forgiven for his sin, Adam was not. "*Mechaseh fisha'av lo yatzliach,*" "One who covers up his sins will not be successful,"[6] but *Hashem* has mercy on one who admits his mistakes.

Another issue is that we think that there is no reason for us to do *teshuva*; overall, we feel that we're doing just fine. We look at ourselves like a man looks at his reflection in the mirror – he takes a quick glance and gets a generally positive impression, and he's ready to go. Really, however, we should scrutinize ourselves like a woman analyzes every detail of her reflection. Just as she looks closely at her makeup and analyzes her outfit, we need to look at ourselves critically and honestly with the intention of improving. This self-analysis is the beginning of the process of *teshuva*. The Sforno notes that only after "*vehashevosa el levavecha,*" you have looked in your

---

2. *Hilchos Teshuva* 2:6.
3. *Yerushalmi, Ta'anis* 2:1.
4. *Bereishis* 3:12.
5. *Shmuel II* 2:13.
6. *Mishlei* 28:13.

heart and faced the truth, is *"veshavta ad Hashem Elokecha"*[7] possible. A person should not be complacent and accept that he is, all in all, doing pretty well.

Another obstacle to proper *teshuva* is that we think that it is unnecessary, as our good deeds will certainly counterbalance the bad. In fact, however, *teshuva* is necessary regardless of our *zechuyos*. The *midrash* writes that *Hashem* told Reuven that since he was the first person to do *teshuva*, repenting completely after moving his father's bed, he was *zocheh* to a descendant – Hoshea HaNavi – who declared, *"Shuva Yisroel ad Hashem Elokecha"* and led *Klal Yisroel* to do *teshuva*.[8] According to *Chazal*, both Adam and Kayin, who lived long before Reuven, also did *teshuva*. Why, then, does the *midrash* refer to Reuven as the first to have repented for his sins? The Ksav Sofer explains that neither Adam nor Kayin had a choice; they had to do *teshuva*. Adam was given only one commandment, and he violated it. He had no other good deeds to balance his sin, so *teshuva* was his only recourse. Kayin murdered his brother, and no good deed could possibly outweigh such a horrendous act, so he, too, had no other choice but to do *teshuva*. Reuven, however, did have a *zechus* to stand in his stead; he had saved Yosef's life when his brothers wished to kill him. He could have felt that it was not necessary for him to do *teshuva* because his good deed far outweighed his evil one. Since he repented nonetheless, he is considered the first to have done *teshuva*. We learn from Reuven that we must repent for every misdeed; we cannot count on our good deeds counterbalancing our sins.

Analyzing our actions, regretting our sins, and resolving to change are all part of the process of *teshuva*, but the process cannot end there. *Chazal* tell us, *"Bo letaher misayin oso"* – if one comes in order to become pure, *Hashem* helps him.[9] It is not enough to want to

---

7. *Devarim* 30:1.
8. *Yalkut Shimoni, Vayeshev* 142; see *Hoshea* 14:2.
9. *Yoma* 38b.

purify oneself; one must "come" to purify himself. Similarly, *Hashem* declares, "*Pischu li pesach kechuda shel machat*" – all a person must do is give *Hashem* an opening the size of the eye of a needle, and then *Hashem* will help him succeed further in his *teshuva*.[10] The Kotzker Rebbe notes that although the eye of a needle is very small, it goes entirely through the needle. *Hashem* asks for a small change, but it must be a real change – through and through.

Although change is necessary we are not expected to make major changes overnight. As *Chazal* teach, "*tafasta meruba lo tafasta*."[11] If one tries to do too much, he often ends up having accomplished nothing at all. We need to provide *Hashem* with a small opening, and He will help us to do the rest.

The story is told that Napoleon once went to visit wounded enemy soldiers in the hospital. He first approached the bed of a Polish soldier and asked him if he had any requests. The soldier asked the emperor to please pull his troops out of Poland and grant the Poles freedom. Napoleon listened intently and told one of his officers to record the request; he would see what he could do. Napoleon next approached a Russian soldier and asked if he had any requests. The Russian asked Napoleon to please liberate Mother Russia. Again, the emperor asked his officer to write the request down and he would see what he could do. Finally, he stopped at a Jewish soldier's bed and asked him if he had any requests. The Jew replied that he would love to have a hot piece of kugel. Napoleon turned to his officer and told him to go to the local store and bring back a piece of kugel for this man. The other soldiers were astonished. Why did the Jew ask for something so insignificant when he had an opportunity to ask for whatever he wanted from the great emperor? He explained, "At least I got what I asked for!"

---

10. *Shir HaShirim Rabba* 5:2.

11. *Sukka* 5a.

Some goals are entirely unrealistic and unattainable all at once. *Hashem* prefers that we accomplish something small and real, rather than make major resolutions that amount to nothing.

In fact, once a sinner makes a small change in his life, he builds momentum that propels him forward to complete self-change. The *gemara* notes an apparent contradiction between two *pesukim*.[12] On the one hand, "*Ki lo achpotz bemos hameis*,"[13] *Hashem* does not desire the *rasha*'s death. On the other hand, "*Ki chafetz Hashem lehamisan*,"[14] *Hashem* desires his death. *Chazal* resolve the contradiction: "*kan b'osin teshuva, kan beshe'ein osin teshuva*." When a person does *teshuva*, *Hashem* no longer desires his death. Rav Yisroel Salanter notes that the word "*osin*" is in the present tense. *Chazal* are telling us that *Hashem* wants to spare "one who **is doing** *teshuva*." Someone who gave himself an initial small push and is now in the process of moving forward is on his way to complete repentance, and *Hashem* does not desire his death.

If a person does *teshuva* properly, he is no longer the same person when the process is complete. The *midrash* notes that the *korban musaf* of Rosh Hashana is described differently than the *korbanos* of the other *yomim tovim*.[15] While all other *korbanos* are commanded with the word "*vehikravtem*," the *korban* of Rosh Hashana is commanded with the word "*v'asisem*."[16] On Rosh Hashana, we are created anew; it is as if *Hashem* made us – "*v'asisem*" – once again. Indeed, the Rambam describes a true *ba'al teshuva* as an "*ish acher*."[17] *Teshuva* totally transforms a person.

---

12. *Nidda* 70b.
13. *Yechezkel* 18:32
14. *Shmuel I* 2:25.
15. *Yalkut Shimoni, Pinchas* 29:2.
16. *Bamidbar* 29:2.
17. *Hilchos Teshuva* 2:4.

During the *Aseres Yemei Teshuva*, we must resolve to set out on the path to *teshuva* and to make the first tiny move, creating a small opening so that *Hashem* will help us to reach even greater heights. Despite the obstacles in our way, we beseech *Hashem*, "*Hachazireinu biseshuva shleima lefanecha*" – "Return us to You in perfect repentance."

The Thirteen *Middos*

After the *chet ha'egel*, *Chazal* tell us, "*Hashem* wrapped Himself in a *tallis* like a *shaliach tzibbur* and showed Moshe the order of prayer. He said to him, "Whenever *Klal Yisroel* sins, let them perform this order and I shall forgive them."[1] *Hashem* assured us that the Thirteen Attributes that He taught Moshe are the key that opens the gates of mercy in every generation. In fact, Rabbi Yehuda states that a *bris* exists concerning the Thirteen Attributes, guaranteeing their effectiveness forever. For this reason, we recite the *Yud Gimmel Middos Shel Rachamim* numerous times during the *Selichos* and the *Aseres Yemei Teshuva* as we ask *Hashem* for forgiveness.

Why do *Chazal* specifically describe *Hashem* as a *shaliach tzibbur* when He recited the Attributes? This suggests that when we *daven*

---

1. *Rosh Hashana* 17b.

to *Hashem*, we should feel a communal responsibility and not be focused solely on our personal needs. We must *daven on* behalf of all of *Am Yisroel* just as a *shaliach tzibbur* represents the entire *kehilla* in his *tefillos*.

Moreover, *Hashem* "wrapped Himself (*nisatef*) in a *tallis*," also symbolizes an essential part of the procedure that must be followed to obtain forgiveness. In *Tehillim*, the same root is used to refer to a poor person who is so ashamed of his poverty that he "wraps" himself in order to hide.[2] When we beg *Hashem* for forgiveness, we must similarly hide ourselves in shame, recognizing that we are essentially empty-handed. "*Velanu boshes hapanim*," we say in the *Selichos*. We are ashamed because we have no good deeds or merits in our favor.

Interestingly, the letters of the word *teshuva* are the same letters of the word, *busha*, as shame is an integral part of repentance. If our child or student misbehaves but feels guilty about it and expresses his embarrassment, we are certainly more inclined to forgive him for his actions. If he is self-righteous and defensive, on the other hand, the response will generally be more severe. Similarly, *Chazal* teach, "Whoever sins and is embarrassed is forgiven."[3] When *Hashem* sees that we "hide ourselves" under the *tallis*, we merit forgiveness and mercy.

How is it possible that merely reciting the Thirteen Attributes of Mercy helps us to attain forgiveness? The *Reishis Chochma* notes that the *gemara* does not say that *Am Yisroel* should say the Thirteen Attributes – "*Imru lefanai*" – but rather that they should "perform" them – "*ya'asu lefanai keseder hazeh*."[4] We are not told to simply mouth the words of a magic incantation, but rather to act in accordance with *Hashem*'s attributes of mercy. The ultimate goal is "*vehalachta*

---

2. *Tehillim* 102:1 – "*Tefilla le'ani ki ya'atof.*"

3. *Brachos* 12b.

4. *Reishis Chochma, Sha'ar HaAnava* 1.

bederachav," to walk in the ways of *Hashem*.[5] If we emulate *Hashem*, acting with *rachamim* and *erech apayim*, then He will act accordingly in dealing with us. The recitation of the Thirteen Attributes teaches us to be compassionate and kind, charitable and slow to anger, to empathize with the plight of a friend, a neighbor, or even a stranger in need or who is suffering.[6]

There is a famous Chassidic story that brings out the idea of "performing" the *yud gimmel middos*. Yankel the *Misnaged* was visiting Sassov during the *Yamim Noraim*, and he noticed that the Rebbe, Rav Moshe Leib Sassover, arrived in *shul* after *Selichos* had concluded. He confronted the Rebbe's followers and asked how a Rebbe could possibly miss *Selichos*. The *Chassidim* responded that the Rebbe was late because he had ascended to the heavens to *daven* on behalf of *Klal Yisroel*.

Dissatisfied, Yankel decided to investigate on his own. The next morning, he followed the Rebbe, who was dressed as a peasant. He watched as the Rebbe walked into the woods, chopped a tree into firewood, and then took the bundle of wood to an old, run-down house. When a woman opened the door, the Rebbe, pretending to be a peasant, said that he had brought the woman wood and food. The woman said she had no money to pay. Rav Moshe Leib told her to pay whenever she had the money. The Rebbe then placed the wood in her furnace and recited the Thirteen Attributes: "*Hashem, Hashem, Keil, Rachum veChanun.*"

---

5. *Devarim* 28:9.

6. If we want *Hashem* to employ these attributes of mercy and compassion, we need to incorporate His kindness and mercy into our lives. It is incumbent upon us to have a clear idea of the meaning of each *midda* so that it can serve as a practical guide for our own behavior. For a detailed explanation, see the *sefer Tomer Devora* by Rav Moshe Cordovero, which offers guidance as to how to integrate each *midda* into one's interpersonal relationships in order to effectuate their power.

Later, when the *Chassidim* asked Yankel if he had seen the Rebbe ascend to the heavens, he responded, "Yes, high into the heavens – if not higher."

When we recite the *Yud Gimmel Middos* during the *Aseres Yemei Teshuva*, we must make a conscious decision to relate to people just as *Hashem* relates to us – with *rachamim*, patience, and tolerance. If we learn to live these Thirteen Attributes of Mercy, we will partake of the abundant wellsprings of *Hashem*'s mercy, and thus merit receiving *selicha*, *mechila*, and *kapara*.

Tzedaka

Shlomo HaMelech teaches us one of the methods of assuring that we will be inscribed in the Book of Life: "*Tzedaka tatzil mimaves*," "Charity saves from death."[1] Why does specifically *tzedaka* have this power?

The Maharal explains that since "*ani chashuv kemeis*," a destitute person is considered as if dead, one who gives a poor person charity is considered as if he physically revived him. In exchange for giving the poor person life, *Hashem* grants life to the *ba'al tzedaka*.[2]

Alternatively, one who donates his hard-earned money to the poor essentially contributes part of his life to the *ani*. After all, it takes time to earn money – hours and hours of one's life. If one wastes that money, he basically throws away all that time he spent earning it; if

---

1. *Mishlei* 10:2.
2. *Maharal Bava Basra* 9B.

he gives that money to those in need, he gives of his own life to the poor.³ In return, *midda kenegged midda*, *Hashem* grants him more life.

Tzedaka indeed has the power to save one's life. In 1912, Nathan and Isadore Strauss – two wealthy brothers who owned the Macy's department store chain and were among the greatest philanthropists in America – travelled to Palestine and toured the region. When Nathan saw the degree of poverty there, he resolved to remain to see how he could help. While Isadore continued on to England on the next leg of their journey, Nathan was engrossed in establishing soup kitchens, medical centers, and schools. He was so engrossed, in fact, that he missed the ship that was to take him and his brother back to America – the Titanic. He was spared the fate that his brother shared with 1,500 others because of his charity. "*Tzedaka tatzil mimaves!*"

Interestingly, Nathan's Hebrew name was Natan, which means, "to give." The word itself is a palindrome – it can be read the same way in either direction – indicating that when a person gives to others, *Hashem* gives to him in return.⁴

Chazal tell us that the *mitzva* of *tzedaka* is equal to all of the 613 *mitzvos* combined.⁵ Thus, on Rosh Hashana, when all of our *mitzvos* and *aveiros* are placed on the scales, *tzedaka* is a tremendous asset, adding weight to our *mitzvos*. Why is the *mitzva* of *tzedaka* considered so "weighty"? One interpretation is that when one gives a poor person money to provide for his basic needs, such as food and medicine, he gives him the strength and ability to perform *mitzvos*

---

3. While the rest of the world maintains that "time is money," we recognize that "money is time"!

4. The city of Netanya was named for Nathan Strauss in appreciation for his generosity. "Netanya" also means "G-d gave." This name is particularly appropriate, as Nathan gave the poor in *Eretz Yisroel* the means to go on with their lives, and *Hashem* granted him life in return.

5. *Bava Basra* 9b.

and learn Torah. As a result, the donor receives a share in those *mitzvos*, and his own *mitzvos* "pile" grows accordingly.[6]

Tzedaka is particularly powerful during the *Aseres Yemei Teshuva* because it is precisely what we ask for from *Hashem*. In our *Selichos*, we emphasize that *"kedalim U'chirashim dafaknu dilosecha"* – we knock on *Hashem*'s door like beggars, beseeching Him for salvation. In *Avinu Malkeinu*, we plead, *"Asei imanu tzedaka vachesed,"* "Treat us with charity and kindness." Since we have no merits, we beg *Hashem* that He grant us *tzedaka*, fulfilling our requests even if we are undeserving. If we demonstrate this attitude towards others, providing them with their needs even if we owe them nothing, then *Hashem* will treat us accordingly.

The Maharam MiPano, a famous kabbalist, noted that the *"At-Bash"* equivalent of the word *tzedaka* – replacing each letter with the corresponding letter at the other end of the alphabet – is *tzedaka* written backwards.[7] Whatever charity a person gives is bound to return to him in the form of *tzedaka* from *Hashem*.[8]

The story is told of two brothers – Chaim, who was quite wealthy, and Moshe, who was abjectly poor. Moshe, in desperate need of funds and with no other choice, decided to approach his brother for help. He travelled to Chaim's office and asked the receptionist to tell him that his brother wished to speak to him. A few minutes later, the receptionist returned and reported that Chaim said that he did not have any brothers. Moshe was devastated; he realized that Chaim was refusing to help him.

Later, when Moshe visited his father, he told him what had happened. The next time Chaim came to visit his father and the older man opened the door, he said, "Who are you? I don't recognize you!"

---

6. *Sefer Ben Yehoyada.*
7. In *At-Bash*, *alef* becomes *taf*, *bet* becomes *shin*, etc.
8. *Ma'amar Chikur Din* 3:20.

Chaim said, "What do you mean? I'm your son, Chaim!" His father responded, "I have a son, Moshe, and he told me that you said that you are not his brother. If that is the case, then how can you be my son?"

In encouraging us to perform the *mitzva* of *tzedaka*, the Torah refers to the poor man as "*achicha*," "your brother."[9] One must give to his fellow Jews just as he would give to his brother. After all, we all share the same father – *HaKadosh Baruch Hu*. Indeed, how can one beseech *Hashem* during the *Yomim Nora'im* as "*Avinu Malkeinu*" if he does not recognize that his fellow Jews are his brothers? If he feels no relationship with other Jews, and therefore no responsibility towards them, then why should *Hashem* take His father relationship into account?

If we open our hearts to our poor brothers, *Hashem* will surely treat us like His beloved children. We will then merit that He will respond favorably to our plea, "*Avinu Malkeinu, chadesh aleinu Shana Tova!*"

---

9. *Devarim* 15:7.

Summary of Ten Ideas to Win the "Court Case"

➤ Dan Lekaf Zechus

Chazal teach us that if we judge others favorably, Hashem will treat us in the same manner. Hashem will take into account our personal circumstances and not judge us exclusively by the letter of the law so that we will merit a favorable judgment.

➤ Zechus of the Tzibbur

If one does not have enough merits as an individual to win the court case, he has another opportunity to be judged as part of society. It is important to be an integral part of society, helping and lending a hand to others. This way, we will be deserving of another year of life because of the others who need us.

➤ Shana Sherasha Betchilasa

As we begin the New Year, we must recognize that we are starting from scratch. We must feel as if we have no family, friends, health or money and we are now asking to be granted these favors again. Just because we possessed these gifts last year, does not mean that we will receive them again this year. Chazal teach us that if we begin the year feeling poor, recognizing that we have nothing, Hashem will grant us all our needs.

➤ Ma'avir Al Midosov

If we overlook other people's indiscretions, Hashem will overlook our *aveiros*. Chazal teach that one who is *ma'avir al midosov* will be forgiven for all his sins.

➤ Kol Hamerachem Al Habrios

Hashem promises us that if we have compassion on others, He will reciprocate. We are surrounded with opportunities to help the unfortunate; let us get involved in doing for others so that Hashem will in turn, have mercy on us.

➤ Simcha

The act of performing a mitzva with joy will increase the value of the mitzvah. In addition, happiness and enthusiasm are contagious and will encourage others to want to do mitzvos. Through our happiness, we will influence others and thus increase our merits.

➤ Tefilla

During this zman, when the gates of tefilla are open 24/7, we must recognize that all that we have comes from Hashem and He is in control of our destiny. This realization will help us to daven a *"tefilla shleima"*, the type of tefilla that Hashem wants and accepts. When making requests, we must keep in mind how having our wishes granted, will improve our *avodas* Hashem.

➤ Teshuva

Repentance can wipe our slate clean. It is a process, not a magic formula that achieves instantaneous results. It involves analyzing our actions, repenting our sins and resolving to change. We must only begin on a course of action at this time of year and that will give us the impetus to continue throughout the year.

The Thirteen Attributes of Mercy

Even though Chazal teach us that through the *Yud Gimmel Middos*, we will merit forgiveness, it is not enough to just recite these attributes. We must incorporate them into our daily lives. We must follow in the ways of Hashem, demonstrating patience, mercy and tolerance for others so that we will merit a *"shana tova umesuka"*.

Tzedaka

As we focus on how to be written in the book of life, we must remember the words of Chazal, *"tzedaka tatzil mimoves"*. Charity will save from death. In *Selichos*, we describe how we appear before Hashem, *"kdalim u'chirashim"*, like paupers, empty handed requesting charity. When Hashem sees us giving *tzedaka* to others, He will in turn be charitable to us.

Rosh Hashana: The Original Mother's Day

On many secular calendars, there is a day specially designated as "Mother's Day," a day on which people focus on the role of mothers. Rav Shimon Schwab *zt"l* writes that the Jewish People observe Mother's Day on Rosh Hashana.[1] Each time the *shofar* is sounded during *Musaf* on Rosh Hashana, we proclaim in unison, "היום הרת עולם," "Today the world was conceived." Rav Schwab notes that while the Hebrew terms for day, week, and month – יום, שבוע, and חדש – are all in the masculine form, the Hebrew word for year is in feminine form – שנה. He explains that days, weeks, and months are merely building blocks forming the year; 24 hours add up to a day, 7 days make a week, and 52 weeks comprise a year. Thus, in

---

1. *Selected Speeches*, pp. 109-119.

a sense, the shorter periods of time are the "offspring" of the year and the all-inclusive year is like the "mother." Since the world was conceived on Rosh Hashana and this day represents the coming year, Rosh Hashana is, in a sense, Mother's Day.

The *Sefer HaToda'ah* also draws a connection between Rosh Hashana and mothers.[2] He explains that one of the reasons that we blow 100 blasts of the *shofar* on Rosh Hashana is that on this day, we must all view ourselves as mothers about to give birth. The *midrash* describes that a woman on the birthing stool cries out 100 times.[3] Her first 99 cries are because she fears she is about to die; her final cry is due to her realization that she is going to live. Similarly, the first 99 *shofar* blasts are blown because of our fear of the judgment, while the final blast is due to our confidence that *Hashem* will judge us favorably. Yeshaya HaNavi describes a pregnant woman who is about to give birth: "She trembles, she cries out in pain – so are we in front of You, *Hashem*."[4] On the Day of Judgment, we are suspended in a state of doubt, as the Books of Life and Death are opened and we wait for our names to be inscribed in one or the other. We do not know whether to laugh or cry. This mixture of fear and confidence that we experience is similar to the emotions of a mother about to give birth.

Since Rosh Hashana is the Mother's Day of the world and on this day we are compared to mothers, it is no coincidence that there are eight different mothers who are associated with this holy day. Chava, the first mother, was created on Rosh Hashana; the *teruah* blasts on Rosh Hashana remind us of the whimpering of Sisra's mother; and Sara, Hagar, Chana, Penina, Rivka, and Rochel are mothers who are mentioned on this day, either in the *machzor* or in the Torah reading.

---

2. *Tekias Shofar – Me'ah Kolos.*
3. *Midrash Tanchuma, Tazria* 1:4.
4. *Yeshaya* 26:17.

A mother's job is unique. No other job requires as much strength, intelligence, patience, and dedication as motherhood. We can understand the significance of the role of a mother from an incident recorded in *Tanach* concerning Dovid and his wife, Michal.[5] When Dovid brought the *aron* up to Yerushalayim, he danced wildly in front of it. When Michal saw Dovid "מפזז ומכרכר," leaping and dancing, she rebuked him for behaving in a way unbefitting a king in front of his "אמהות," his maidservants. The *midrash* says that King Dovid responded that these women were not maids (*amahos*), but rather mothers (*imahos*).[6] The *midrash* concludes that Michal was punished for criticizing Dovid with these words; as the *pasuk* states, she did not have a child until the day of her death.[7] The Radak interprets this to mean that she died in childbirth.

Michal perceived Jewish mothers as maids who clean, cook, and change the diapers. Dovid told her that they are not maids – they are mothers. Being a mother does not only mean bearing a child; it means molding and shaping a child. A mother creates the daily atmosphere in the home, which determines her family's spiritual direction. She doesn't instruct, but rather lives and models the Torah. This is the noblest job a woman can have. Since Michal did not recognize the loftiness of a mother's role, she lost the opportunity to bring up a child.[8]

The Munkatcher Rebbe was once traveling in a wagon during a heavy snowstorm. Strong winds knocked down the signpost at one of the crossroads that the wagon had reached, and the wagon driver was lost; he had no idea which way to turn. He got out of the wagon and lifted the signpost from the ground. It was marked with four different destinations, each with an arrow pointing in a different direction.

---

5. *Shmuel II* 6:20.
6. *Bamidbar Rabba* 4:20.
7. See *Shmuel II* 6:23.
8. Rav Meir Bergman, *Sha'arei Orah*.

The wagon driver planted the sign back in the ground, returned to his wagon, and continued driving. The Rebbe was astounded. "How did you know which way to place the sign if you did not know where to turn?" The driver responded, "I knew the direction of Munkatch, where we came from, so I placed the sign with the arrow facing Munkatch. All the other arrows then fell into place!" The Rebbe was impressed. "This is a very valuable lesson for life," he declared. "When a person knows where he is coming from, he will know in which direction he is heading."

The mothers from our past who are associated with Rosh Hashana transmit important messages to us that can be instrumental in helping us prepare for the coming year. If we look back to where we came from and examine the lives of these mothers, we will surely glean many worthwhile lessons from them. As we incorporate that inspiration into our personal lives, we will be steered in the right direction for the upcoming year.

In this *zechus*, may all our *tefillos* be accepted and may we be inscribed in the Book of Life for a *shana tova umesuka*.

Chava

Although Chava is not mentioned in our Rosh Hashana *tefillos* or Torah reading, she was created on the very first Rosh Hashana of the world, and we therefore consider her to be one of the mothers of the day.

Immediately after Adam and Chava were informed of their punishment for eating from the forbidden fruit, Adam named his wife "Chava," because she was the "אם כל חי," the mother of all living things.[1] Chava had caused Adam to sin by enticing him to eat the fruit, and as a result their lives would never be the same. Imagine how broken, dejected, and distressed Chava must have felt at the time! She probably thought to herself that she was supposed to be a "עזר כנגדו," a helpmate to Adam, and instead she had made his life more difficult! Adam understood and he encouraged her and lifted her up.

---

1. *Bereishis* 3:20.

He showed her that he still respected her; he built up her confidence and self-esteem by calling her "the mother of all living things." He gave her the ultimate compliment, the greatest title – "mother." He showed her that a person can make a mistake, and even fail, but still retain his intrinsic value.

I was once invited to speak to a group of students who were studying in a *yeshiva* for boys who were struggling. I began my presentation by taking out a crisp, new $50 bill and I asked, "Who wants this bill?" All hands shot up. I proceeded to crumple the bill. I then held it up again and repeated my question. They were all still interested. I placed the bill on the floor and stomped on it and dirtied it, and then I offered it again. They did not change their minds; they all wanted the $50 bill. I then asked, "Why do you want it? It looks pathetic! It's squashed, dirty, and disgusting." They answered that it still has the exact same value of $50 as when it was brand new. I explained to them that when a Yid sins and sullies himself, no matter how low he has fallen, his value remains the same. *Hashem* still loves him the same way. Sin is just an outer layer; every Jew is pure inside.

Nosson DeTzutzisa is an example of a person who fell to the lowest depths and was able to rise to the greatest heights.[2] Rashi explains that Nosson received the title "*Tzutzisa*" – meaning spark or light – because a light shone upon him like Moshe Rabbeinu. Nosson wanted to act immorally with a married woman and his desire was so strong that it made him physically sick. He once had the opportunity to be with this woman, but he overcame his strong *yetzer hara*. In that *zechus*, a light emanated from his face. This man was none other than the great *Amora* Mar Ukva.[3] Shmuel refers to him as "*Reishei dereishoch*," "the head of the head," the highest in the *yeshiva*.

---

2. *Sanhedrin* 31b.

3. *Shabbos* 55b.

We must remember that we each have great potential. *Hashem* loves and respects every one of us. As Bila'am said, "לא הביט און ביעקב"[4] – *Hashem* does not focus on the sins of Yaakov. Rashi comments that even when a person rebels and angers *Hashem*, He doesn't leave him. On the contrary, the *posuk* concludes, "ותרועת מלך בו," "the friendship of *Hashem* is with him."

The Purim story illustrates this point clearly. The Jews sinned by eating at the party of Achashverosh. Haman then rose to power and made a decree to annihilate the Jews. The Yidden did *teshuva* and were saved. The miracle that saved the Jews actually began at Achashverosh's party, when Vashti was killed, paving the way for Esther to become the new queen. At the same time that the Jews were sinning at the party, *Hashem* was preparing the miracle to save them! This demonstrates how great *Hashem's* love is for us.

The reason that *Hashem* loves us can be learned from a *medrash*.[5] When Yaakov dressed in Esav's garments and came to receive the *brachos* from Yitzchak, the *posuk* tells us that Yitzchak smelled "בגדיו," his clothing.[6] The *medrash* comments that this word should be interpreted as "בוגדיו," "his traitors." Through *ruach hakodesh*, Yitzchak smelled the future traitors of the Jewish People.

The *medrash* relates the story of one such traitor. When the Romans came to destroy the *Beis HaMikdash*, they asked a Jew named Yosef Mishisa to show them around the *Beis HaMikdash*. As payment for his assistance, he was permitted to take whatever he wanted from the Temple. He went in and took the golden *menora*. When he came out holding the *menora*, the Romans told him that the *menora* is not for a commoner to use and that he should go back in and choose something else. He refused. He said, "It is enough that

---

4. *Bamidbar* 23:21.
5. *Medrash Rabba* 65:22.
6. *Bereishis* 27:27.

I already angered *Hashem* once." They tortured him to death, and all the while he screamed, "Woe to me that I angered *Hashem*," crying in *teshuva*. This man had reached rock-bottom. He was ready to take the golden *menora* for himself. He realized how low he had fallen when he saw that even the *goyim* understood the *kedusha* of the *menora*, while he did not. He then did *teshuva shleima*, and *Hashem* accepted his repentance. The *medrash* explains that Yitzchak Avinu could smell that even the rebellious among us, such as Yosef Mishisa, have a spark deep inside that can be ignited.

If this is what the *pasuk* is trying to tell us, why does it actually say "בגדיו," "clothing," and not "בוגדיו," "his traitors"? Rav Yaakov Galinsky *zt"l* explained that rebelliousness is similar to clothing. Garments are external; they are not part of the person and can easily be removed. Similarly, our sins are just a covering that can be removed. *Hashem* sees each individual for who he really is, the person underneath the externals, and that is the one He loves. As Zechariah says, "הסירו הבגדים הצאים מעליו," "remove the filthy garments from him"[7] – in other words, remove his sins.

Mistakes are an essential part of growth. All of the 39 forbidden actions on Shabbos are acts that were necessary for the building and use of the *Mishkan*. When were writing and erasing used in the *Mishkan*? The *Mishkan* was dismantled and rebuilt repeatedly, so letters were written on the wooden beams to indicate which boards were to be placed where. Sometimes a wrong letter was mistakenly written on the posts and it was necessary to erase them to correct the errors.[8] Obviously, not every action that the builders took when building the *Mishkan* is included in the list of the forbidden *melachos*. After all, the builders of the *Mishkan* drank glasses of water and handed objects to one another, yet these actions are not included in the Shabbos prohibitions! Only activities that were an integral

---

7. *Zechariah* 3:4.

8. *Shabbos* 103b.

part of the construction of the *Mishkan* are prohibited on Shabbos. Since erasing is one of the 39 forbidden actions, this must mean that "erasing" is an indispensable part of building.

In truth, errors are part of the project of life itself, which bears heavily on the concept of *teshuva*. It is through repeated falls that a person truly achieves righteousness. Struggles, including failures, are inherent to the achievement of eventual victory. Therefore, when a person fails or makes a mistake, he should not despair.

As Rosh Hashana approaches, it is easy to get depressed and think, "It is hopeless! I have sinned too many times." People tend to feel overwhelmed by their personal spiritual failures. We must keep in mind and remember the lesson that Chava teaches us. Even when we slip up, *Hashem* still loves and respects us because our essence is pure.

Sarah

On the first day of Rosh Hashana, the Torah reading is about Sara *Imeinu*, the first Jewish mother. For 90 years, Sarah waited for a child, until finally, "וה' פקד את שרה," "*Hashem* remembered Sarah."[1] Avraham named the child Yitzchak, and both he and Sarah were overjoyed that they had been blessed with a son.

Sarah observed Hagar's son, Yishmael, being "מצחק,"[2] acting frivolously, and she demanded that Avraham expel him from their home. Rashi explains that the term "מצחק" is a euphemism for the three cardinal sins – idolatry, illicit relations, and murder. It seems that Sarah observed Yishmael committing these severe crimes, and she therefore demanded that he be removed from her home so that he would not have a harmful effect on Yitzchak's moral development.

---

1. *Bereishis* 21:1.
2. *Bereishis* 21:9.

This incident is puzzling. If Yishmael actually committed these acts, why would the Torah obscure them by using the ambiguous term "מצחק" rather than being more explicit? Furthermore, why was Avraham loath to send Yishmael away? He clearly did not want to raise his son Yitzchak with a murderer, philanderer, and idolater any more than Sarah did!

Perhaps Rashi does not mean that Yishmael had **already** committed these transgressions. Rather, Sarah saw Yishmael's frivolous attitude, his scorn of anything significant – the fact that he was "מצחק" – and she recognized that these were seeds that would ultimately fester to become a debased personality capable of performing appalling acts. She anticipated the future and demanded immediate action.

Bear in mind that Sarah was not a cold, detached woman. After all, she ran the household that serves as the model of *hachnasas orchim* (hospitality) for all times. She and her husband created a home that is the very paradigm of the *middah* of *chesed*. *Chazal* tell us that Avraham converted the men and Sarah converted the women.[3] She hosted all sorts of unsavory guests, many of whom were idolaters and pagans; she certainly must have been very tolerant and understanding of all types of people and personalities. But this same model of *chesed* expelled her own stepson from her home! She so clearly saw who Yishmael was and what he would become that she insisted that he be sent away immediately – and *Hashem* agreed with her assessment.

Shlomo HaMelech teaches, "חכמת נשים בנתה ביתה," "The wisdom of women builds a home."[4] *Chazal* define "wisdom" as the capacity to foresee the future.[5] Women are blessed with ability to see deeper, to look with a clearer vision at what the future will bring, and that vision

---

3. See Rashi, *Bereishis* 12:5.
4. *Mishlei* 14:1.
5. *Tamid* 32a.

ultimately builds the home. Sarah saw that Yishmael's seemingly insignificant mischief had major ramifications for the future, and she was proven right.

The same is also true in the reverse. Often, even minor acts of goodness have significant ramifications. I personally experienced this at a *Shabbos Nachamu* event in a hotel at which I delivered some *shiurim* on Shabbos, including the *Daf Yomi shiur*. The *daf* of that Shabbos was a particularly difficult one. After I finished the *shiur*, one of the guests approached me and inquired when I would be teaching Sunday's *daf*. I informed him that I had not been asked to deliver a *shiur* on Sunday and I intended to leave on Sunday morning immediately after *davening*. He said that he was relying on me, but I merely shrugged my shoulders and excused myself. But then I began to think. One day this *Yid* is going to come before the Heavenly court. The defending angel will say that he was diligent in Torah learning and finished all of *Shas*. The prosecuting angel will negate his words and declare that the man never completed *Shas* because on the 14th of Av, 5771, he skipped the *daf*. The defending angel will respond that it was not the man's fault; Menachem Apter is to blame for the missed *daf*! After this thought occurred to me, I went back to the man and agreed to learn with him on Sunday morning before *Shacharis*. And wouldn't you know – ten people showed up! The consequences of my actions were more far reaching that I could have imagined. I thought that I was helping one person, but in reality, ten people benefited from my one small act.

Often, the impact of our actions is the greatest when we realize it the least – when other people learn from our simple activities. Rav Matisyahu Solomon related a story about a famous Rosh Yeshiva in *Eretz Yisroel* who became a *ba'al teshuva* because of one such "small" act. This man had been living on a kibbutz; he knew absolutely nothing about Yiddishkeit and was even anti-religious. In fact, he was one of the most depraved people on the kibbutz. One day, he heard about an immoral place of entertainment that had recently opened. At the first opportunity, he rode there on his motorcycle. While parking, he saw a *frum* Jew passing the building and turning his head to the side in order not to see anything indecent. The Rosh Yeshiva related that when he saw this passerby look away, he was shocked! He had been planning this trip for weeks; he was so excited, and this man wasn't even interested! He wondered, "What does he have that is more enticing than this place?" He decided to find out. He looked into Yiddishkeit, became a *ba'al teshuva*, and eventually became a Rosh Yeshiva of thousands of students.

Rav Matisyahu added insight to the story. Imagine what will happen when this man who looked away comes before the Heavenly court. They will honor him and give him a seat among all the *gedolim*. He will say, "There must be a mistake! This can't be my seat!" But they will tell him, "There is no mistake! You deserve to sit here because you taught so many students!" He will respond, "But I was a simple electrician! I never taught a day in my life!" And they will explain that since the Rosh Yeshiva became a *ba'al teshuva* because of his action, all the Rosh Yeshiva's students are also considered his own. Of course, he will not recall ever having made anyone a *ba'al teshuva*. When they tell him about how the fact that he turned his head was the catalyst that brought the Rosh Yeshiva to the path of Yiddishkeit, he will certainly not even remember the event. But that simple, seemingly insignificant act had powerful repercussions.

Our words also have significant ramifications that we may not realize. A story is told about the Chofetz Chaim, who was staying at an inn and was eating his meal with another man. The owner came over and asked if they were satisfied, and the Chofetz Chaim's companion said everything was fine but the food was too salty. The owner apologized. After he walked away, the Chofetz Chaim rebuked his companion. "Maybe the cook is a widow, the mother of orphans, and this is her only source of income. What happens if she gets fired because of what you said?" The man replied, "You're getting carried away. All I said was that the food was salty!" The Chofetz Chaim walked towards the kitchen and motioned to the man to join him. The man was horrified to see the owner berating the cook. "I've told you numerous times to be more careful. You're fired!" The woman burst into tears. "I am the sole supporter of my family. How will we survive?" The man ran over to the owner and begged him not to fire the cook; he would do anything to help her keep her job. He had only intended to critique, not to ruin anyone's life!

A similar story is told about two seminary girls who were sitting on a bus and indulging in some *lashon hara* about another girl in their seminary. Each one had a negative comment about her. The entire time, a woman sitting behind them was listening to their conversation. As the girls prepared to get off the bus, she turned to them and said, "Thank you so much for all the information! My son was supposed to get engaged to your friend tonight. Imagine what a tragic mistake that would have been! We will call it off right away!" The girls turned white. "We didn't mean it! We were exaggerating! Please, please, don't do it!" They were beside themselves and they didn't know what to do to rectify their mistake. The woman told them to relax. "My son is not really getting engaged to your friend – but he could have been! Next time, think before you speak!"

We should learn from Sara *Imeinu* to think ahead and consider every action we take and every word that we say. We must always keep in mind what the consequences of our actions and speech will be.

Hagar

Hagar is mentioned in the same Rosh Hashana Torah reading as Sara. Realizing that it was unlikely that she would be able to bear children for Avraham, Sarah suggested that he take her maidservant, Hagar, as a wife. Hagar gave birth to Yishmael, and he was raised in the home of Avraham. After Sarah miraculously gave birth to Yitzchak, she recognized that Yishmael was not a proper influence on her child, who would be the scion of *Hashem*'s nation, and she told Avraham to send Hagar and Yishmael away.

The Torah tells us, "וישלחה ותלך ותתע במדבר," "And he sent her and she went and she wandered in the desert."[1] *Rashi* comments that upon leaving the house of Avraham, Hagar returned to the practice of idol worship of her father's home. The *Sifsei Chachamim* questions how *Rashi* learns this from the words of the *posuk*. The *posuk* states

---

1. *Bereishis* 21:14.

that Hagar wandered in the desert; it does not mention anything about worshipping *avoda zara*.

We can explain this with a story that is told about R' Mordechai Pogromansky (known as R' Mottel). R' Mottel was traveling on a train together with a friend who was a *shochet* and a *mohel*. They were so engrossed in their conversation that they missed their stop, and they had no choice but to get off at the next stop, an unfamiliar location. When they disembarked, it was very close to Shabbos and they had no idea where they were. R' Mottel's companion was terrified. What would they do? Where would they stay for Shabbos? R' Mottel reassured his friend, "A Jew is never lost! If we are here, it is not because we are lost; it is because we are meant to be here!"

The two men made some inquiries, and they were told that there was one Jewish family living in the small town. The travelers hastily approached the home and knocked on the door. The man who opened the door was visibly excited to see the two Jewish men standing before him. He invited them inside and asked, "Is it possible that one of you is a *mohel*?" R' Mottel's friend answered, "I am a *mohel*. But how did you know?" The host smiled and explained that his wife had given birth to a baby boy on the previous Shabbos. He was unable to take his wife and baby to a larger city where the *bris* could be performed and he was unable to arrange for a *mohel* to come to them for Shabbos. He *davened* that *Hashem* would help him make the *bris* in its proper time. When the two strangers knocked on his door, he knew that *Hashem* must have sent a *mohel* to him! R' Mottel reminded his friend of what he had told him before – a Jew is never lost.

Rav Elya Meir Bloch expressed this idea in a speech he delivered on the occasion of the laying of the cornerstone of the Telz Yeshiva in Cleveland. The *Navi* records that when Dovid was unsure if it was safe to go to Shaul's Rosh Chodesh *seuda*, Yonasan arranged a sign to let Dovid know. Yonasan would shoot three arrows in Dovid's direction and he would send his lad to fetch them. If he would tell the boy that the arrows were beyond him, then Dovid would know, "כי שלחך ה'," "that *Hashem* has sent you away."[2] Why didn't Yonasan simply say that Dovid would know to run way? Why did he express the same idea in this vague manner? Rav Bloch explained that Dovid understood that a Jew is never on the run. If he has to run, it means that *Hashem* is sending him somewhere else for now. Similarly, Rav Bloch explained that he had not fled Europe. Rather, "*Hashem* has sent me from Europe to Cleveland because He wanted me to help build a yeshiva here!"

This idea may help us to understand how Rashi deduced that Hagar returned to idol worship. The *posuk* writes "ותתה במדבר." Hagar wandered in the desert; she was lost. Describing Hagar as lost is the equivalent of saying that she severed her connection with *Hashem* and lacked belief in His Divine guidance. A true believer in *Hashem* never takes a wrong turn and is never lost. Even if he had different intentions of where to be or plans of where to go, he always finds himself in the situation that was Divinely predestined for him.

In the Torah reading on Rosh Hashana, we learn further about Hagar's state of belief after leaving Avraham's home. When there was no more water in her flask, Hagar despaired and left Yishmael to die. A *malach* appeared to her and told her that her son would survive, and in fact would be the father of a great nation. *Hashem* made a miracle and a spring of water appeared in the dry desert, "and she went and filled her water pitcher and gave the boy to drink."[3] The *Midrash* tells us that we learn from here that Hagar was lacking in *emuna*. She did not take just enough water to save her son, but rather filled her flask; she prepared for later and did not trust that *Hashem* would continue to provide for her and her child.

---

2. *Shmuel I* 20:22.
3. *Bereishis* 21:19.

This comment of the *Midrash* is difficult to understand. In what way do Hagar's actions reflect a lack of *emuna*? After all, she had a sick child and wanted to be sure that she would have enough water for him. Why does this show a lack of faith?

Rav Leib Chasman explains this *Midrash* through a *mashal*.[4] If a person were invited to travel with a benevolent and kind king, the traveler would obviously not need to bring along tuna sandwiches and drinks. Indeed, if he were to take food with him on the trip it would be considered an insult to the king! His actions would indicate a lack of appreciation for who the king is and the fact that he can certainly provide for the needs of a fellow traveler. Similarly, after witnessing the miracle of a spring being created for her in the barren desert, Hagar should not have felt a need to take extra water with her. *Hashem*, the benevolent King, was taking care of her; there was no reason to worry about the future. Her worrying demonstrated a lack of *emuna*.

The lesson that we can learn from Hagar is that a Yid should never feel lost or alone. *Hashem* is always with us, no matter what. Franklin D. Roosevelt famously declared that "There is nothing to fear but fear itself." For a Jew, there is nothing to worry about but worry itself! Worrying is a sign of a lack of *emuna*. Dovid HaMelech makes this point succinctly: "השלך על ה' יהבך"[5] – throw your *pekel*, all of your worries and concerns, to *Hashem* and let Him take care of them!

The story is told of a Rav who was travelling on a plane and noticed a young girl sitting not far from him who was travelling alone. Suddenly, the pilot made an abrupt announcement. "Severe turbulence is expected. Please fasten your seat belts. No food or drinks will be served." The plane began to shake violently, and all of the travelers became anxious. People were screaming, but the little

---

4. *Ohr Yahel, chelek* 3, *Vayera*.
5. *Tehillim* 55:23.

girl continued coloring as if nothing was wrong. The plane abruptly dropped fifty feet, causing luggage to fall out of the overhead bins. Many passengers began to pray; the Rav started to recite *Tehillim*. Everyone on the plane was terrified – but the girl remained calm in her seat. Eventually, the flight returned to normal and the passengers landed safely at their destination. As they were disembarking, the Rav asked the little girl, "Weren't you afraid when the plane was shaking and luggage was falling all around you?" "No," she responded. "My daddy is the pilot. I knew he would get me home safely."

As we approach Rosh Hashana, we should remember that *Hashem* is our father and our pilot, and He will guide us to safety, no matter the current turbulence.

Sometimes, *Hashem*'s guidance and closeness is not obvious to us, but the truth is that He is always present by our side. The story is told of a man who experienced many difficult times. Whenever he was struck by misfortune, he felt as though *Hashem* had left him on his own. He would lift his eyes up to Heaven and say, "קלי קלי למה עזבתני," "My G-d, my G-d, why have you abandoned me?"[6] One night, he dreamed that he was walking on a path. When he looked behind him, he saw two sets of footprints, but when the path narrowed, he saw only one set of footprints. He realized that this represented the path of his life – from birth through childhood, youth, middle-age, and old-age. When the path was wide and times were good, *Hashem* was travelling by his side, but when the path narrowed and times were difficult, *Hashem* was not there. During the hard times, he had to manage on his own. The man cried out, "Why *Hashem*? Why did you leave me when I needed you most?" He heard a gentle voice answer, "My dearest child, you are mistaken. Yes, in difficult times, you seemed to be walking alone, but in reality, I was even closer at that time. When all was going well, I walked beside you, helping and encouraging you. But when the path became narrow, during the

---

6. *Tehillim* 22:2.

trying times, there was no need for a broad path, as I did not walk beside you. I carried you on my shoulders."

As Dovid HaMelech said, "גם כי אלך בגיא צלמות לא אירא רע כי אתה עמדי," "Even when I walk in the valley of the shadow of death, I fear no evil, for You are with me."[7] If we learn the lesson from Hagar, we will strengthen our *emuna* in *Hashem* and realize that we are never lost; He is always there, by our side or carrying us.

---

7. *Tehillim* 23:4.

The Mother of Sisra

Another mother connected to Rosh Hashana is *Eim Sisra*, whose name we do not know. Sisra was the general of Yavin, king of Canaan, who attacked *Eretz Yisroel* during the leadership of Devorah and Barak. The Jews defeated the Canaanim, and Sisra was killed by Yael. In the song that Devorah sings after the victory, she describes Sisra awaiting her son's return from battle. As time passes, her despair grows: "ותיבב אם סיסרה: מדוע בשש רכבו לבא," "The mother of Sisra cried, 'Why is his chariot late in coming?'"[1] Tosfos explains that we blow 100 blasts from the *shofar* on Rosh Hashana in order to nullify the 100 cries of the mother of Sisra. These 100 *kolos* serve as a *meilitz yosher*, a defense for us on the Day of Judgment.[2]

---

1. *Shoftim* 5:25.
2. *Rosh Hashana* 33b.

Who was Sisra? The *midrash* relates that he was a mighty warrior who conquered the world at age 30 and could knock down walls with his war cries. There were millions of troops under his command, yet he was defeated in battle by the 10,000 soldiers led by Devorah and Barak. *Chazal* explain that the word "בשש" ("delayed") is a contraction of two words, בא שש – six hours have come. Normally, Sisra would win his battles in three or four hours, and now six hours had passed and his mother was concerned.

Why were the tears of *Eim Sisra* so powerful that they require us to counteract them with our *shofar* blasts? After all, Sisra was no hero fighting to protect his homeland. Like many before and after him, his only goal was "להשמיד להרוג ולאבד את כל היהודים," to annihilate the Jewish People. Why must we counteract a woman's tears for this *rasha*? Indeed, she doesn't seem like such a pleasant individual herself. When she cried, her maidservants tried to comfort her by assuring her that he was killing the best and brightest of *Klal Yisroel*, dividing the spoils and attacking the young girls – and *Eim Sisra* doesn't show any sympathy for her son's innocent victims. She only worries about her son! Why are we concerned over the power of the tears that an evil woman shed for her evil son?

Rav Isser Zalman Meltzer taught that we see from here the power of tears. Even these wicked tears need 100 blasts to wipe them out! Often, our words and our thought are not connected. We can be speaking about one thing and our mind is elsewhere. When we cry, however, our thoughts and cries are synchronized; there is no disparity between our tears and our mind. A person may *daven* while thinking about an entirely different matter than he is asking for, but a person does not cry about one issue and think about something entirely different. Because tears are so focused, they are powerful, and this is the reason that we need to negate the tears of *Eim Sisra*.

How do we know that *Eim Sisra* cried 100 times? Rav Isser Zalman explains that the total number of letters in the *posuk* describing her crying is 101. We only blow 100 blasts, and not 101, because her first cry was not the same as the others. The first cry was before her maidservants comforted her. It was a cry from the depths of her heart, the heart of a mother in pain and distress for her child. The next 100 cries were from a despicable heart, a heart full of evil and wickedness, a heart comforted by the thought of the plundering and killing of innocent men, women, and children. Those cries we can undo, but the cry of a mother in pain for her child is so powerful that even the *shofar* cannot erase it. That cry remains forever.

If the cries of *Eim Sisra* have such power, imagine the effect of the tears of a Yiddishe Mama crying for her children! R. Mattisyahu Solomon relates a story that took place in the Gateshead Yeshiva that demonstrates the power of a mother's tears.[3] As in all *yeshivos*, there was great competition among the boys to get the best *chavrusos*. Every student sought to get the best learning partner possible. One particular boy, despite being a serious student, was of average intelligence and was not a shining star. The other boys knew this, and they all expected him to settle for less than the best *chavrusa*. Why would the brightest and most talented choose him? However, for some reason, this boy always found an exceptional partner. None of the staff or the students could understand how he accomplished this. Even the boys who agreed to learn with him could not explain why they had done so. Usually, these partnerships would only last one semester. Nonetheless, to everyone's amazement, this boy would find another first-rate *chavrusa* the following semester. It was baffling.

One day at the beginning of a semester, a *Rebbe* overheard the boy speaking on the phone to his mother. "Ima," he said, "you can stop *davening* now. I got my new *chavrusa*. He is first-rate, one of the best." Now everything became clear. It was only through his mother's heartfelt prayers and tears that this boy was able to always find the top *chavrusa*!

---

3. *With Hearts Full of Faith*, p. 96.

Since tears are so powerful, we must be extra careful with them. Crying over nothing can be compared to a surgeon using his scalpel to engrave his name on a tree. Something so valuable should not be wasted on something so trivial! When the *meraglim* returned with their negative report about *Eretz Yisroel*, *Klal Yisroel* cried a *bechiya l'chinom*, tears for no reason, and they were punished with a *bechiya l'doros*, tears for all generations. They cried for nothing, and they were punished with something to truly cry about. That fateful day became a day of tragedy, a day of mourning – Tisha B'Av.

This brings to mind a story about a woman who lost her child. The mother could not be consoled. She stopped going out of the house and did not attend any celebrations. One day, she was supposed to attend the wedding of her best friend. Her husband felt that she should really attend, as it would mean so much to her friend, but she felt she could not possibly be happy. After much persuasion, her husband succeeded in convincing her to go to the wedding.

When she arrived at the hall and heard the music playing and saw the people dancing wildly, the woman burst into tears. An old woman who was sitting outside the hall and collecting *tzedaka* approached her and asked her what was wrong. The bereft mother responded that she recently lost her child and she simply could not get over her loss. The elderly woman said, "I understand your pain. I lost my entire family during the war." "Didn't you cry?" the younger woman asked. The elderly woman answered, "Yes. I cried and cried, and then I realized that these precious tears were being wasted. They would not bring back my family. So instead of crying for my own pain, I began to cry for others. I cried for the people who had no children. I cried for sick people and I cried for others who were suffering."

When the bereaved woman heard these words, she sat down and cried copious tears for all the people she knew who were in pain. When she finished, she dried her eyes, stood up and walked into the hall and began dancing. She had never felt happier in her life. Her tears would no longer be wasted.

The *gematria* of בכי, crying, has the same numerical value as לב, heart; tears and the heart are intertwined. Crying raises the level of our pleas to a new dimension. We often don't realize the power of our *tefillos*. We should learn from the mother of Sisra how powerful a plea from the depths of the heart can be. Let us use our tears properly when we daven. May we then be *zocheh* to the fulfillment of the *posuk*, "הזורעים בדמעה ברינה יקצרו."[4] Those who plant heartfelt cries of *teshuva* and *tefilla* will reap the fruits of those seeds in a life filled with sweetness, happiness, and *bracha*.

---

4. *Tehillim* 126:5.

Chana

On the first day of Rosh Hashana, we read the story of Chana in the *haftora*. Chana was barren, and every year she came to the *Mishkan* to cry her heart out. Chana's prayers were finally answered on Rosh Hashana, when she gave birth to a son who grew up to become the great *navi* Shmuel.

Chazal learn many *halachos* of *tefilla* from the prayer of Chana.[1] The *Navi* describes, "וחנה היא מדברת על לבה," "And Chana, she was speaking from the heart."[2] *Chazal* learn from here that one must *daven* from the heart and concentrate when praying. Indeed, this is the essence of prayer. For this reason, prayer is described as "*avoda shebalev*," service of the heart, not of the mouth.[3]

---

1. *Brachos* 31a.
2. *Shmuel I* 1:13.
3. *Ta'anis* 2a.

Immediately before Chana went to pray in the *Mishkan*, her husband Elkanah said to her, "למה תבכי?... הלוא אנכי טוב לך מעשרה בנים?," "Why do you cry?... Am I not better to you than ten sons?"⁴ The next *pesukim* describe, "ותקם חנה... ותתפלל על ה'," "Chana got up... and prayed to *Hashem*."⁵ What inspired her to daven at that particular moment? The Malbim explains that until that point, she had been relying on the *tefillos* of her husband, who was a *tzaddik*. Now she realized that he had given up hope, and she decided that she must therefore *daven* for herself. We learn from here not to put our trust in others; we must put all our faith in *Hakodosh Baruch Hu*, the source of all blessing.

This reminds me of a story of a simple couple who had not been blessed with children. Someone told them of a holy and pious Rebbe who lived in a distant village. The Rebbe was known to be a miracle worker. The couple gathered a sum of money to give to the Rebbe, as is the custom when asking for a blessing, and they set on their way. When they were admitted to the Rebbe's private chamber, they poured out their hearts and begged him to confer his blessings upon them and promise them a child. The Rebbe said, "I can do it for you for 150 gold coins."

Although the couple had prepared a large sum of money, this amount was way out of their ballpark. It represented more than their life's savings! They told the Rebbe that they would gladly donate generously, but they were not rich people; they could not possibly afford such an exorbitant sum. But the Rebbe refused to back down. He insisted on 150 gold coins; otherwise, there would be no blessing.

Upon hearing the Rebbe's unreasonable demand, the husband became angry. He turned to his wife and said, "Who needs this Rebbe

---

4. *Shmuel I* 1:8.

5. *Shmuel I* 1:9-10.

anyway? *Hashem* is great enough that He can give us His blessings without this Rebbe and his golden coins!"

As the couple stormed out, the Rebbe turned to a disciple and said, "They will be blessed with a child. At first, they put their trust in me, so I could not help them. A Rebbe can give a blessing, but a blessing is simply a form of prayer. Before seeking blessings, one must recognize that all blessing and goodness flow from *Hashem*; only then can the blessing have an effect."

Even though Chana suffered for many years, she never gave up hope. Dovid HaMelech instructs us, "קוה אל ה׳, חזק ואמץ לבך וקוה אל ה׳," "Hope to *Hashem*; strengthen and fortify your heart and hope to *Hashem*."[6] *Chazal* learn from the repetition of the word "קוה" that if one *davens* and is not answered, he should *daven* again.[7] Interestingly, the word used to describe *tefilla* in this *pasuk* is "קוה," "hope." When one *davens*, it must be with *bitachon*, trust in *Hashem* and continuous hope that one's prayers will be answered. Chana never gave up hoping, and *Hashem* responded to her *tefillos*.

A woman once travelled to an annual fair to buy a year's supply of materials for the family store. On the first day of the fair, she realized that she had lost her bag with all the money for her purchases. She panicked and began to cry uncontrollably. Suddenly, someone approached her and told her that a man in one of the stands had found the money. The woman was delighted and rushed over to ask the man for her money. The man, however, refused to give it to her. He told her that according to the *halacha*, if one loses something in a place filled with mostly *goyim*, one is *meya'esh*; he gives up hope, and thereby relinquishes ownership of the money. The man had no obligation to return the money to her.

---

6. *Tehillim* 27:14.

7. *Brachos* 32a.

The woman was devastated and insisted that the man come with her to ask Rav Yitzchok Elchonon Spektor for his opinion. When the Rav heard the story, he told the man that he must return the money. The man reluctantly gave the woman the sack of coins, but he questioned the Rav. "Why must I return it to her if she gave up hope? It is now mine!" The Rav explained that the money did not belong to her; it was her husband's. The fact that she gave up hope had no bearing on the situation. She could not give up hope on something that did not belong to her. Since her husband had no idea that the money was lost, he had never given up hope, and the money therefore still belonged to him.

When Rav Yeruchem Levovitz, the *mashgiach* of the Mir Yeshiva, heard this story he used it to teach a lesson in a *mussar shmuz* that he gave to the *yeshiva bochurim*. In *Selichos*, we declare, "הנשמה לך והגוף שלך" - our *neshamos* and our bodies belong to *Hashem*. We stress this same point every day during the period of the *Yamim Nora'im* when we recite the *perek* of *L'Dovid Hashem* and say, "'אחת שאלתי מאת ה."[8] Tosfos writes that the word "אחת" can refer to the *neshama*.[9] Thus, the *pasuk* can be interpreted to mean, "I have borrowed (שאלתי) my *neshama* (אחת) from *Hashem*." Our bodies and souls do not belong to us, but rather to *Hashem*. Therefore, Rav Yerucham said, we can never give up hope on our *neshamos*; we must constantly strive for growth.

This is a powerful lesson that we learn from Chana. Despite the fact that she saw Penina give birth to ten children while she remained barren, she continued to *daven*. She never gave up hope, and her *tefillos* were eventually answered.

Rav Elya Lopian learns a similar lesson from a perplexing *gemara*. Rav Meir describes a case of two people who are sick with the same illness. Both men *daven*, but only one is answered. The difference,

---

8. *Tehillim* 27:4.

9. Tosfos, *Menachos* 18a.

Rav Meir explains, is that one man *davens* a "*tefilla shleima*" and the other does not. Rashi explains that a *tefilla shleima* is a prayer said with *kavana*.[10] But how is it possible for a man who is at death's door not to *daven* with *kavana*? As he *davens* to *Hashem* – "Please save me! Don't let my wife become a widow and my children become orphans! Please allow me to walk my children down to the *chupa*!" – is it possible that at the same moment he is thinking about the stock market or where to go on vacation?! Is it feasible for anyone in this dire situation to not be *mechaven*?

Rav Lopian explains that in this context, *davening* without *kavana* means praying and not believing in the effectiveness of the prayer. He doesn't expect his prayers to be answered; he has given up hope. If that is true, why does he *daven* at all? Perhaps he prays to gain merit in the next world or in the unlikely chance that it will help, but deep down, he really doesn't believe that his prayers will make a difference. This is not a *tefilla shleima* and will not be effective.

Sometimes, a person who is saying *Tehillim* for a sick person cries tears of sadness, but not tears of hope. A *tefilla* must be said with faith, hope, and confidence that *Hashem* is all powerful and can accomplish anything.

Chana teaches us another important lesson about *davening* as well. When she beseeches *Hashem* to grant her a child, her request is not for personal or selfish reasons, but rather for the privilege of raising a son who will dedicate his life to one purpose – serving *Hashem*. This is indicated by the *pasuk* describing her prayer. Instead of writing, "ותתפלל אל ה׳," that Chana *davened* to *Hashem*, the *pasuk* says, "ותתפלל על ה׳"[11] – she *davened* for the sake of *Hashem*.

---

10. *Rosh Hashana* 18a.
11. *Shmuel I* 1:10.

We all enter Rosh Hashana with a laundry list of desires. But why should *Hashem* grant our requests? Are we worthy? We must daven like Chana – *al Hashem*, for the sake of *Hashem*. As we ask *Hashem* to inscribe us for life, health, *parnassa*, and all our other needs, we must add that if our *tefilla* is successful, these blessings will help us serve *Hashem* better. We ask, "זכרנו לחיים...למענך אלקים חיים" – we *daven* that *Hashem* will grant us life not for our sake, to live a life of pleasure, but rather for His sake, in order to serve Him better. Only when we dedicate our existence to fulfilling the task that *Hashem* has set for us do we have the right to ask for life.

Jewish mothers have often exemplified this trait of Chana. I heard a story from Rav Dovid Engel, a *menahel* in Toronto, about one such woman. A *yeshiva* was on the verge of closing down due to its precarious financial situation. After many warnings, parents who failed to pay tuition were told that their children would be sent home and would not be allowed to stay in school if they didn't pay. One third grader, an orphan, arrived home with a note: "We are aware of your situation and do not expect you to pay the tuition. However, we need to clearly demonstrate how desperate the situation is. Please keep your son home for three days and then you can send him back to school." The boy returned to school the next day with a note in an envelope. It read, "Dear Administration, I cannot allow my son to remain home for even one day. טוב לי תורת פיך מאלפי זהב וכסף![12] Enclosed is the engagement ring that my late husband *z"l* gave me. Please use it to pay my son's tuition. Please don't force my son to miss even one day of Torah learning!" This courageous woman followed in Chana's footsteps. Her whole purpose in life was *lema'ancha*, for *Hashem*.

As we approach the *Yemei HaDin*, we should emulate Chana; we should never despair and keep *davening* "*al Hashem*," for *Hashem*'s

---

12. *Tehillim* 119:72.

sake, not for ourselves. Let us truly feel, "אבינו מלכנו עשה למענך אם לא למעננו," "Please, *Hashem*, answer us for Your sake, if not for ours."

Penina

Penina, appears briefly in the *haftora* of the first day alongside Chana. Elkana had two wives; Penina was blessed with children, but Chana was not. The *pasuk* describes, "וכעסתה צרתה גם כעס," "Her rival [co-wife] would provoke her again and again."[1] *Chazal* explain that Penina would taunt Chana, "Did you buy a coat for your older son or a shirt for your younger one?" She did not do this out of malice, however. In truth, she wanted to pain Chana in order to inspire her to daven more.[2] Penina succeeded in her mission, as Chana indeed *davened* after being provoked, and she was then blessed with a son, Shmuel.

Although Penina's actions were *leshem shamayim,* with the best intentions, they nevertheless caused Chana much pain and

---

1. *Shmuel I* 1:6.
2. *Bava Basra* 16.

suffering. Penina was severely punished for causing pain to Chana. In the song that Chana sings after her salvation, we read, "עד עקרה ילדה שבעה ורבת בנים אמללה," "Until the barren woman bore seven and the one with many children was bereft."[3] In the end, Chana was blessed with children, while Penina's children died. Rashi comments that we are told that Chana had only five children. Why does the *pasuk* mention seven? Rashi cites Rabbi Yehuda, who relates that every time Chana gave birth, two of Penina's children died, so by the time Chana had four children, Penina had only two left. When Chana had her fifth child, Penina begged her to *daven* that her two remaining children would not suffer the fate of their siblings. Chana did so and they survived. Thus, Chana was credited not only with her own five children, but also with two of Penina's children, who were saved due to her prayers.

Rav Chaim Shmulevitz questions why Penina was punished so harshly when she was simply trying to help Chana. He explains that one must view causing pain to another as a burning fire. Even if a person puts his hand in fire accidentally, his hand will still get burnt. Similarly, if a person irritates another person, even unintentionally and even with altruistic motives, he is still held accountable for the aggravation that he caused.[4] This teaches us how careful and sensitive we must be with another person's feelings. There are no excuses! As they say in Yiddish, "*Nebech er meint es ernst.*" The equivalent expression in English is "The road to *Gehinnom* is paved with good intentions."

One must go to great lengths to avoid embarrassing another person. One *seder* night, the Sar Sholom of Belz, the first Belzer Rebbe, was sitting next to his elderly mother. She broke a piece of *matza* and put it into her soup. The Chassidim looked on in horror, as they are very strict concerning avoiding *gebrokts*, eating wet *matza*

---

3. *Shmuel I* 2:5.

4. *Sichos Mussar Maamar* 24 *Korach* 5731

on Pesach. When the Rebbe's mother noticed their looks, she began to feel uncomfortable. The Rebbe sized up the situation, picked up a spoon, and ate some soup from his mother's plate, even commenting on the wonderful taste. Later, he explained to his Chassidim that *gebrokts* is just a *minhag*, but honoring one's mother is a *mitzvah min haTorah*.[5]

Causing pain to others always has repercussions. Yosef sent his son, Menashe, to chase after Yosef's brothers and accuse them of stealing his cup. When Menashe confronted them, they ripped their clothing from grief. Rabbeinu Bachayei writes that because Menashe caused them to tear their clothing from heartache, *midda kenegged midda*, his tribe's inheritance in *Eretz Yisrael* was "ripped apart" – one half was in *Eretz Yisrael* proper and the other half was across the *Yarden*.[6] Even though Menashe was fulfilling a *mitzva* by obeying his father, he was punished for causing distress to his uncles. His noble purpose did not help him avoid punishment.

The Vilna Gaon finds a hint to this idea in the *pasuk* warning us not to cause pain to a widow or orphan: "אם ענה תענה אתו, כי אם צעק יצעק אלי שמע אשמע צעקתו," "If you cause him pain, if he calls out to me, I will surely hear his cry."[7] The word "כי" seems superfluous; it would have sufficed to say "אם צעק יצעק אלי." The Vilna Gaon explains that in this context, "כי" means "so that." In other words, if you cause pain to the widow "so that" she will cry, I will listen to her cries. You may not cause pain to someone even if you think it is for the other person's benefit!

It is very easy to fall into the trap of doing the wrong thing even when one is well-meaning and acting *leshem shamayim*. The story is told of a man who came home from *shul* Friday night and found

---

5. *UMatuk HaOr*, Yom Kippur, p. 193.
6. Rabbeinu Bechayei, *Bereishis* 44:12.
7. *Shmos* 22:22.

that the *challos* were uncovered. He berated his wife, and although she tried to explain, he would not listen. Eventually the couple went to their Rav to help them restore harmony in their home. The husband mentioned his wife's lack of adherence to *halacha* in leaving the *challos* uncovered. The Rav smiled and said to him, "When both wine and bread are on the table, we usually recite the *bracha* of *HaMotzi* before the *bracha* of *HaGafen*. Since on Shabbos we must make *Kiddush* and drink the wine before we say *HaMotzi*, we cover the *challos* so as not to embarrass them. We are so sensitive even to the feelings of inanimate objects such as *challos* – how much more considerate should you be not to embarrass your wife!"

Sometimes, a person's thinking becomes so warped that he thinks that hurting another person is actually a *mitzva*. When Yaakov met Rachel, he cried because he came empty-handed, without any gifts. Rashi tells us that Eliphaz, the son of Eisav, had chased after Yaakov with the intention of killing him. When he was about to kill Yaakov, he found that he simply couldn't do it, as he was raised in Yitzchak's home. He asked Yaakov, "What should I do about the command of my father to kill you?" Yaakov responded, "Take all of my possessions; then I will be penniless, and a poor person is considered dead." Rav Chaim Shmulevitz points out that it is possible for a person to become so confused that he thinks that there is a *mitzva* to murder someone. Eliphaz thought he was fulfilling a *mitzva* by following his father's command, and even when he refrained from doing so, he felt uncomfortable![8]

This reminds me of one of my *talmidim*, who took upon himself to recite *Perek Shira* every day as a *zechus* for a *refuah* for a sick woman who lived in his neighborhood. I noticed that he was saying it during *Kaddish* and *Chazaras HaShatz*. I had a difficult time convincing him that it is not a *mitzva* or a *zechus* for the lady if he is

---

8. *Sichos Mussar Maamar* 7, *Vayetzei* 5733

davening for her during these important times. It is better not to say it at all!

Even if we do not err to the same degree as Eliphaz, we are certainly liable to make Penina's mistake. From Penina we learn that we must analyze the *mitzvos* that we do and make sure that they are truly *mitzvos*. Good intentions alone are not enough!

Rivka

Rivka is hinted to in the morning *tefilla* of *Shochen Ad*. This *tefilla* is recited every Shabbos and Yom Tov, but on Rosh Hashana, *nusach Ashkenaz* rearranges the words to match those of *nusach Sefard*. The *nusach* on Rosh Hashana is "בפי ישרים תתרמם ובדברי צדיקים תתברך ובלשון חסידים תתקדש ובקרב קדשים תתהלל." The first root letter of every third word in this *tefilla* spell out the name רבקה. In most *machzorim*, these letters are written in bold type to hint at Rivka's name, and she is thus incorporated into our Rosh Hashana *davening*. Rivka's birth is also mentioned at the end of the Torah reading on the second day of Rosh Hashana.

We learn from Rivka how to do *chesed* properly. When Eliezer wished to test Rivka to see if she would be a suitable wife for Yitzchak, he asked her for a drink. She not only responded graciously, declaring, "I will give you and your camels to drink," just as Eliezer had stipulated in his test, she also added, "until they finish drinking."[1] She was willing to make a great effort to provide for the needs of both Eliezer and his animals.

The *Beis Halevi* explains that Eliezer was checking to see if Rivka is a kind person who performs *chesed* wisely, in the optimum way. When Eliezer would finish drinking, Rivka would have a dilemma. What should she do with the leftover water? She could not take it home, as a stranger had drunk from it, and she might spread germs and sickness to her family. On the other hand, she could not pour the water on the ground, as that would be an insult to Eliezer. The way to circumvent this problem was to offer the leftover water to the camels. Rivka, however, went one step further. She was concerned that if she offered to give the camels to drink, Eliezer might understand that she was trying to avoid taking the remaining water home, and he would be hurt. She therefore offered to give the camels to drink until they finished drinking, even though that meant she would have to refill her flask many times. This was *chesed* with true *chochma*.

Rivka also performed her *chesed* with modesty. When Eliezer asked Rivka for water, he should have asked for her name and family first, in order to make sure that she was from the family of Avraham. If not, she would be disqualified to be Yitzchak's wife, even if she would give the camels to drink. The *Ksav Sofer* explains that Eliezer didn't ask her for her name first because he wanted to see if she would do *chesed* as an anonymous person, knowing she would not get any recognition. If she had revealed her name and family, she might do the *chesed* just to impress Eliezer, so that he would tell others how wonderful she is.[2]

It is interesting to note that although Rivka is considered one of the mothers of the day, her appearance on Rosh Hashana is almost non-existent. She is hinted to in *davening* and one line is written

---

1. *Bereishis* 24:19.

2. *Ksav Sofer, Bereishis* 24:17.

about her birth in the Torah reading of the day. Perhaps the reason is to teach us that *chesed* must be done with *tznius*, with modesty.

Another trait that we learn from Rivka is that when helping others, one should act quickly, with *zerizus*. When Rivka went to draw the water, the *posuk* describes, "ותמהר... ותרץ, "She hurried... she ran." Rivka rushed to do *chesed*. She did it with alacrity, eagerness, excitement, and passion. That is the manner in which *chesed* and *mitzvos* must be done.

I heard a story that exemplifies these *middos* of Rivka. Miriam's family was having financial difficulties, and she was quite distressed. Her second son was becoming a Bar Mitzva in a few weeks and there was simply no way that they could afford a celebration. Miriam cried to her close friend, Devora. "How can I tell my son that we don't have money to make a Bar Mitzvah celebration? His brother had a beautiful catered affair, and he will have nothing!" Devora told her that she had recently heard that one of the *tzedaka* organizations in the area was running a raffle campaign, and the first prize was a catered party for 100 people in a hall with a photographer and a one-man band. She suggested that Miriam buy a five dollar ticket and *daven* to *Hashem* that she should win. Devora said that she knew where to buy the ticket, so she offered to pick it up for her friend.

Two weeks later, Miriam's *tefillos* were answered. She received a phone call announcing that she was the lucky winner of the first prize. She was in a state of shock. It was a miracle! Bubbling with excitement, she called Devora to share the good news with her and thank her for the brilliant suggestion.

Now I will tell you the rest of the story. There was no raffle. When Devora heard of Miriams's predicament, she wanted to help her, but she knew that Miriam was very proud and would never accept any help. So she made up the story of the raffle, printed a ticket on her computer, and hired the hall, caterer, photographer, and band. Then she arranged for someone to call Miriam and tell her that she had won the raffle. *Mi ke'amcha Yisrael!* This is true *chesed* done with *chochma*, with creativity and common sense, but also with *tznius*. Devora was not looking for any recognition for her good deed.

Chazal tell us that if one has compassion for others, *Hashem* will in turn have compassion on him.[3] We must learn from Rivka how to care for others properly, with wisdom, modesty, and excitement and then, with *Hashem*'s help, we will succeed in arousing *Hashem*'s mercy toward us and He will bless us with a *shana tova umesuka*.

---

3. *Shabbos* 151b.

Rochel

Rochel Imeinu has been crying for her children for the past 2,000 years. On the second day of Rosh Hashana, we read in the *haftora* about how Rochel refuses to be comforted until all of her children, the Jewish People, return safely from exile. *Hashem* tells her that she can stop crying and dry her tears, for He will return the Jewish People to their land.[1]

The *midrash* relates that when King Menashe set up an idol in the *Beis HaMikdash*, *Hashem* made the decision to destroy the *Beis HaMikdash* and exile the Jewish People. At that time, all of the *Avos* came before *HaKodosh Boruch Hu* and pleaded with Him to rescind His decree. Avraham said, "Spare them in the *zechus* that I was willing to sacrifice my beloved son for You!" Yitzchak cried, "Spare them in the *zechus* that I put my neck out, ready to be slaughtered!"

---

1. *Yirmiyahu* 31:14-16.

Yaakov and Moshe came forward as well, but none of their pleas were accepted. Finally, Rochel came forward and said, "Before my marriage to Yaakov, we anticipated that my father Lavan would try to trick Yaakov, and we made secret signs so that Yaakov would know that the bride was truly me. But I gave the secret signs to my sister to spare her embarrassment, and I wasn't jealous of her. So, too, *Hashem*, You should not be jealous when *Klal Yisroel* turns away from You to worship *avoda zara!*" *Hashem* replied with the famous words of the *haftora*, "מנעי קולך מבכי ועיניך מן דמעה כי יש שכר לפעולתך," "Restrain your voice from crying and your eyes from tears, for there is a reward for your actions."[2]

Why did *Hashem* accept Rochel's *tefillos* more than the pleas of the *Avos* and Moshe Rabbeinu, our greatest leaders? What was so unique about her *tefilla* that made it more powerful than even the *zechus* of the *akeida*?

When Rochel gave the *simanim* to Leah, she was giving up her *nitzchius*, her eternity – her role as a mother in *Klal Yisrael*. As far as she knew, Yaakov observed the Torah and would never marry two sisters; she would be forced to marry Eisav. Nevertheless, she was willing to sacrifice her future so as not to cause her sister shame. Rochel and Yaakov had discussed the scenario of Lavan trying to fool them, and they created the signs so that Rochel could be easily identified; Rochel really had no right to renege on the deal and give the signs to Leah. Yet, she couldn't stand idly by and witness her sister's embarrassment. Her love for her sister was too great. Rochel argues, "*Ribbono Shel Olom*, even though *Klal Yisroel* are not deserving of Your mercy, they are Your children. How can You stand by and watch them suffer so greatly?" Because of Rochel's *mesiras nefesh* for her sister, *Hashem* listened to her pleas and will bring the *geula* for *Klal Yisroel*. *Hashem* helps those who care about others.

---

2. *Pesichta Eicha Rabba* 24.

Rochel teaches us that in order to get our *tefillos* answered, we must feel and care deeply about one another. If it really hurts us to see someone else suffer and we are willing to help others even if they are not deserving of our help, then we gain the right to ask *Hashem* to help us with our needs, even if we are not deserving. This is why the Arizal says that one should accept upon himself the *mitzva* of "ואהבת לרעך כמוך," loving one's fellow Jew, before beginning to *daven* in the morning, as this is the key to getting our *tefillos* answered.

One of the greatest reasons for the departure of the *Shechina* from among *Klal Yisroel* is *sinas chinam*, baseless hatred. The converse, *ahavas chinam*, unconditional love for one another, brings the *Shechina* back to *Klal Yisroel*. We learn this from the *keruvim*, the two child-like angel forms that rested on top of the *aron*. The *keruvim* symbolized the love and kindness of one Jew for another. They were found in the holiest place on earth, the spot of the greatest divine presence – the *Kodesh Kodoshim*. This teaches us that when Jews love each other, the *Shechina* is present.

Indeed, love for others is an identifying trait of the Jewish People. When Basya, the daughter of Pharaoh, opened the basket containing Moshe, the Torah tells us, "ותפתח ותראהו את הילד, והנה נער בוכה," "And she opened and she saw him, the child, and behold, it was a young boy crying."[3] Why does the Torah use two different words to describe Moshe – *na'ar*, which connotes an older child, and *yeled*, which refers to a young child? The Baal HaTurim explains that *yeled* refers to Moshe, but *na'ar* actually refers to Aharon, who was standing nearby and crying. The Chidushei HaRim writes that when Basya saw Aharon crying over the fate of his brother, she knew "מילדי העברים זה," "This one is from the children of the Hebrews." She knew that Jews care about and cry for one another; the fact that Aharon was crying for the child indicated that the baby must be Jewish. Just as Aharon cried for his brother and was thereby *zocheh* to help bring *geula*, Rochel

---

3. *Shmos* 2:6.

similarly cries out to *Hashem* to redeem us, and the ultimate *geula* will be in her merit.

A rich businessman once came to the Chasam Sofer and poured out his heart. He was doing poorly in business and needed a *bracha* from the *tzadik*. The Chasam Sofer looked at the man and said, "*V'gam ani shomati*, I have also heard that your brother is destitute and you have not helped him." The man replied that he had a hard enough time worrying about himself. How can he also manage to take care of his brother?

The Chasam Sofer explained that *Hashem* said to Moshe, "וגם אני שמעתי את נעקת בני ישראל," "I have also heard the groaning of *Bnei Yisroel*."[4] The word "גם," "also," is an inclusive term; it always includes something or someone else. *Hashem* said, "I am **also** listening to their groans, to their pain." Who else besides *Hashem* was listening? The answer must be, the Chasam Sofer said, that even though the Jews in *Mitzrayim* were suffering and in pain, they still managed to feel their brother's plight. "גם" is referring to the *Yidden* in *Mitzrayim*, who felt the misery of their fellow *Yidden*. As a result of *Klal Yisroel*'s empathy for one another, *Hashem* also had mercy on them and they were redeemed from *Mitzrayim*. The Chasam Sofer told the businessman that the fact that he was in need did not exempt him from his responsibility towards his brother. He must help him in any way possible, and in that *zechus*, *Hashem* would save him from his troubles. Consideration and concern for others brings about the national *geula* as well as personal redemption.

Rochel Imenu did more than simply care for others. As we saw above, she sacrificed a tremendous amount in order to prevent her sister's suffering. This exceptional form of self-sacrifice of Rochel has been repeated in different generations throughout our history.

---

4. *Shmos* 6:5.

About 100 years ago, there was a young girl in Yerushalayim who was going to *gan* (kindergarten) for the first time. All the other girls were escorted by their mothers, led gently with soothing words of encouragement, but this girl was pulled along by her eight year old brother and left alone in the school yard. She cried hysterically, with no one to comfort her.

That night, Rav Yosef Chaim Sonnenfeld was walking through the streets of Yerushalayim, and he passed the young girl sitting on the stoop in front of her home and sobbing. She cried, "I'm only going to school tomorrow if my mommy takes me!" The Rav asked her, "Why can't your mommy take you?" The girl answered, "My mommy is sick in the hospital." Rav Sonnenfeld responded with a *bracha*, "*B'ezras Hashem*, your mother will take you to the *chupa*," and he walked on.

The girl's mother recovered somewhat and eventually came home. She was always sickly, but there were times when her health improved. The years went by. The little girl grew up and it was time for her to get married. Many *shidduchim* were suggested, but she turned each boy down with a different excuse; one was too tall, one was too short, one had too much money, and one had too little. One day, her father said to her, "You can't delay any longer. It's time for your younger sister to get married!" "Let her get married before me," she said. Her father wasn't happy, but he felt that he had no choice. The conversation repeated itself again and again, as each of her younger siblings got married before her. Finally, when all were married, she accepted a *shidduch* that was not the same caliber of boy that she had been offered many years earlier.

Shortly after her wedding, her mother passed away. At the *levaya*, she finally explained her behavior. "When I was a little girl, the great *tzaddik*, Rav Yosef Chaim Sonnenfeld, gave me a *bracha* that my mother should take me to the *chupa*. I wanted to share this *bracha* with all of my siblings!" This is an example of a girl who followed in the footsteps of our Mama Rochel, willing to sacrifice her needs for the sake of her siblings.

I heard a story about Rebbitzen Etta Rivka Zucker *a"h* of Chicago that illustrates willingness to help others. When her daughter was in seminary, she became close friends with a girl from a very poor Yerushalmi family. After seminary, this girl needed to find work so that her family would have food to eat. She decided to clean houses to earn money. The Rebbetzin's daughter was very upset when she heard that her good friend was forced to take on such a job. One day, the Zucker's cleaning lady quit and they were left without cleaning help. Rebbetzin Zucker's daughter jokingly said to her mother, "Too bad my friend in Yerushalayim can't be our cleaning help!" Rebbitzen Zucker responded, "I will hire her." For the next twelve years, Rebbetzin Zucker cleaned her own house and mailed the money that she would have paid a cleaning lady to the girl in Yerushalayim! Rebbetzin Zucker truly personified the traits of Rochel Imeinu.

If we follow in the footsteps of Rochel and are willing to sacrifice our personal needs for the sake of others, then we will *b'ezras Hashem* be *zocheh* to the comforting words that *Hashem* promised Rochel, "ושבו בנים לגבולם," "and your children will return to their borders." In the merit of our mother Rochel, may we be *zocheh* to the *geula shleima*, speedily in our days.

Summary of Eight Mothers Related to Rosh Hashana

1. **Chava** - Just as Chava sinned and was forgiven, so too, when we sin we should never despair or give up hope. Every Jew is pure inside; sins are just an outer layer that can be removed. Even if we make a mistake and we sin, Hashem loves us and waits for us to do *teshuva*.

2. **Sarah** - Sarah expelled Yishmael from her home because she foresaw the consequences of his frivolous attitude, so too, we must realize and be aware of the impact of our deeds. Small actions, both positive and negative, can have major ramifications for the future.

3. **Hagar** - Hagar was lost and wandering in the desert. Rashi understands from this that she returned to idol worship. We must learn from Hagar's mistake that we should never feel lost; we are alway in the place that was Divinely predestined for us and Hashem is always guiding and watching over us.

4. **Eim Sisra** - Sisra's mother cried 101 tears and we are obligated to negate those tears with our *shofar* blasts. We learn from Eim Sisra that tears are powerful and we must not waste them. Through sincere and heartfelt tears and prayer, we will succeed in having our requests granted.

5. **Chana** - From Chana we learn how to daven properly and never to give up. Chana does not ask for a child for personal reasons, but rather to raise a son who will serve Hashem. So too, when we daven, we must daven for Hashem's sake, to be able to serve Him better.

6. **Penina** - Penina provoked Chana in order to inspire her to daven. From Penina we learn that we must be careful when we decide to do something for altruistic motives. We may have the best intentions, but if someone will be hurt by our actions, we will be held responsible for the pain that we caused.

7. **Rivka** - From Rivka we learn how to perform *chesed* with wisdom, eagerness and modesty. If we show proper kindness to others, Hashem will in turn perform kindness for us.

8. **Rochel** - From Rochel's *mesirus nefesh* toward her sister, we learn that we must sacrifice our personal needs for the sake of others. Hashem promises us that consideration and concern for others will bring the ultimate *geula*. May we be *zoche* to the *geula shleima,* speedily in our days. Amen!

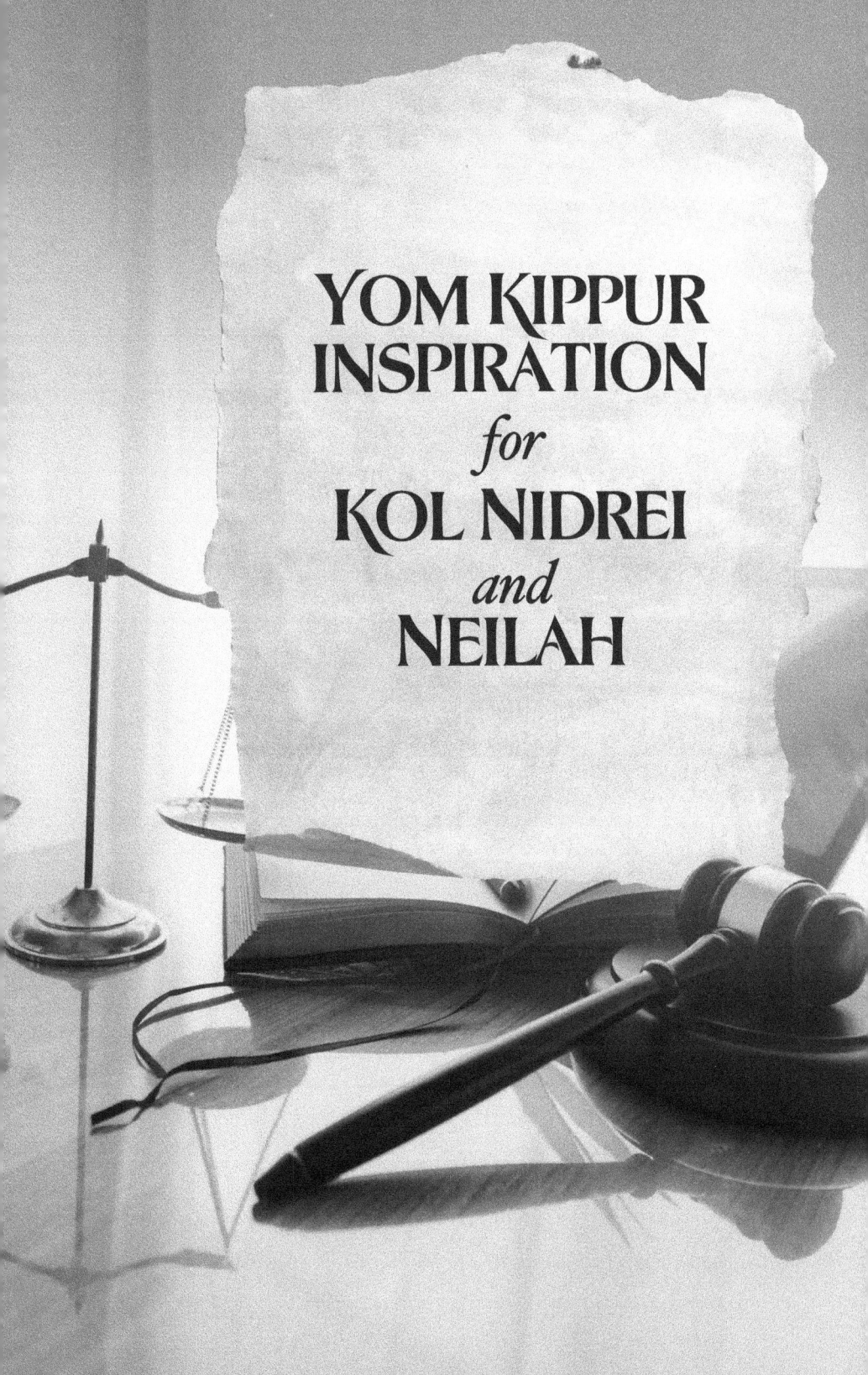

Don't Be Like the Horses

Chazal tell us: "הכל הולך אחר החיתום," "Everything is [judged] based on its conclusion."[1] We have reached *Ne'ilah*, the conclusion of our forty-day *avodah*. It's the climax, and we can all sense the tremendous inspiration.

The *Yerushalmi* brings two opinions regarding the source of this *tefillah*'s name,[2] explaining that it is either a reference to נעילת שער השמים, the closing of the doors of Heaven, or נעילת שער ההיכל, the closing of the doors of the *Beis HaMikdash* as the day's *avodah* concluded.

Nonetheless, as *Chazal* teach us, "שבעים פנים לתורה," "There are seventy ways [in which to interpret] Torah.[3] Perhaps we can suggest

---

1. ברכות יב.
2. ירושלמי ברכות פרק ד הלכה א
3. זוהר בראשית מז:

another reason for the name *Ne'ilah*, which includes a powerful message.

Since the start of Yom Kippur, we have been prohibited from נעילת הסנדל, wearing shoes, and when this *tefillah* ends, we will be permitted to wear our shoes again. Perhaps the word *Ne'ilah* hints to נעילת הסנדל, signaling to us to get ready to put our shoes on. What is the significance of this? After all, we are also going to go home and eat and drink now. Why is it so notable that we will be putting our shoes back on?

The *pasuk* in *Shir HaShirim* describes, "מה יפו פעמיך בנעלים," "Your footsteps were so beautiful in your shoes."[4] *Chazal* explain this *pasuk* to be the words of the other nations, who praised *Klal Yisrael* as they observed them being *oleh regel*.[5] What did the nations notice about this trip that impressed them? And why do they mention the shoes that the Jews were wearing?

When a person went to the *Beis HaMikdash*, he had to remove his shoes. In fact, it was forbidden for a person to wear shoes on the entire Har HaBayis.[6] Similarly, when Hashem appeared to Moshe Rabbeinu at the burning bush, He commanded him, "של נעליך מעל רגליך, כי המקום אשר אתה עומד עליו אדמת קודש הוא," "Remove your shoes from your feet, because the place you are standing on is holy ground."[7]

Why is it necessary to remove one's shoes in a holy place? Rav Chaim of Volozhin explains: "כשם שהנעל מחזיק את הגוף, כך הגוף מחזיק את הנשמה. הגוף הוא נעל לנשמה," "Just as the shoe is a container for [part of] the body, so too, the body is a container for the *neshamah*." The body is the 'shoe' of the *neshamah*." The *neshamah* is not physical; it is not able to walk, and it can't do *mitzvos*. It needs its "shoe" to

---

4. שיר השירים ז:ב.
5. עי׳ סוכה מט:
6. ברכות נד.
7. שמות ג:ה.

help it "move," and that shoe is the physical body. When one comes to a *makom kadosh*, he must remove his shoes, which represent the physical body –*gashmiyus* – and focus entirely on the *neshamah* – the spiritual. One must leave the physical world behind.

Just as we remove our shoes in the holiest place, we remove our shoes on Yom Kippur, the holiest day of the year, when we leave our physical needs behind and become like *malachim*. On Yom Kippur, we transcend the physical world and connect with the spiritual.

When the nations saw *Klal Yisrael* being *oleh regel* and observed how *Klal Yisrael* were reaching great spiritual heights in the *makom hamikdash*, a place that, by its very nature, was above and beyond the physical, they weren't impressed. But when the non-Jews watched the Jews returning to their homes, they noticed that they were wearing their shoes, connecting themselves once again with the physical, but they nevertheless were still holding on to the spiritual inspiration they had attained in the *Beis HaMikdash*. Recognizing this, the nations of the world proclaimed, "מה יפו פעמיך בנעלים," "Your footsteps were so beautiful in your shoes!" They were amazed at how we had returned to the world of *gashmiyus*, yet remained on such a high spiritual level.

Similarly, it is relatively simple to reach a high level on Yom Kippur, the day we remove our shoes and leave the physical body behind. The real test of Yom Kippur is when we put our shoes back on and return to the world of *gashmiyus*. On Yom Kippur, anyone can be a *kadosh*; the question is, did we **absorb** the *kedushah*? Can we now integrate it into our *guf*?

This might explain why the *tefillah* could be named after נעילת הסנדל – because putting our shoes back on is the entire purpose of this *tefillah*. This is the time when we no longer act like *malachim* and we reenter the physical world.

Some Jews, unfortunately, are what we call "Three-Day-a-Year-Jews," the type that come to *shul* only on Rosh Hashanah and Yom Kippur. We shouldn't be Three-Day-a-Year-Jews. Instead, the lessons we take from the *Yomim Nora'im* should remain with us the entire year.

Rav Bunim of Peshischa was once approached by a man who complained that he had fasted forty days in a row, after having seen in the *seforim* that one who does so will merit meeting Eliyahu HaNavi. "I fasted," the despondent visitor moaned, "but Eliyahu never came!"

Rav Bunim responded with a story about the Ba'al Shem Tov:

> After settling in his wagon enroute to a distant destination, the Baal Shem Tov instructed Alexi, his coachman, to drop the horses' reigns and turn around. Alexi complied and took his seat facing the Baal Shem Tov, while the wagon and horses miraculously soared into the sky. The several-week journey was then completed in a matter of hours.
>
> While they flew, the horses noticed that they were passing the feeding stations without stopping. "If we don't need to eat or drink," the horses reasoned, "perhaps we aren't animals. But we can't be humans, because we're flying. We must be *malachim*!"
>
> After arriving at their destination, Alexi unhitched the horses and led them to a barn. As they guzzled water and devoured oats, they looked at each other and nodded in agreement. "Well," they realized, "I guess we are horses, after all."

The idea of fasting for forty days, Rav Bunim told the man, is not for a person to simply get through the fasts and then return to the same place he was before. Fasting is meant to refine a person, to raise him to a higher level. If, the moment the fast ends, he enthusiastically attacks his food with the excitement fitting any other starved individual, he has accomplished nothing, and his fasts will not cause him to merit meeting Eliyahu.

We have not fasted for forty days, but since Rosh Chodesh Elul, we have been involved in a forty-day *avodah*. If, when we put our shoes back on, we dive into the food, if there has been no change in us at all, we aren't very different from those flying horses. As Dovid HaMelech teaches: "אל תהיו כסוס כפרד אין הבין," "Do not be like a horse or a mule that doesn't understand."[8]

Tonight will be the true test of whether we have accomplished anything in the last forty days. We must hold on to the inspiration. We should stop and think before making a *brachah* on food, in order to have the proper concentration and to be grateful to the *Ribono Shel Olam* for providing it. We should be careful how we interact with people.

If we hold on to the inspiration tonight and take it with us, the *malachim* will look down at us and proclaim, "מה יפו פעמיך בנעלים," "How beautiful *Klal Yisrael* is, even when they have left the world of *malachim* and returned to the *gashmiyus* world!" We will then have truly accomplished the purpose of the *avodah* of the last forty days.

---

8. תהלים לב:ט

Beware of the Satan

Chazal note that the *gematriah* of the word השטן is 364, which represents the 364 days of the solar year on which the *satan* is able to prosecute us.[1] The 365th day, when he can't prosecute, is Yom Kippur. In fact, the *midrash* tells us that on Yom Kippur, the *satan* comes before *HaKadosh Baruch Hu* and proclaims, "Look at Your children! They are like *malachim*. They are not eating or drinking, they are wearing white, and they are davening all day!"[2]

This seems rather strange. Even if the *satan* can't accuse *Klal Yisrael* on Yom Kippur, why is he suddenly defending them? Reb Itzele Peterburger explained that, in fact, the *satan* is not defending us at all. His plan is to accuse us right after Yom Kippur, when a sinner

---

1. יומא כ.
2. פרקי דרבי אליעזר מ"ו

will once again defend himself and argue, "What do you want from me? I don't have the strength to obey Hashem to such an extent!" The *satan* will then counter, "On Yom Kippur you managed to! In fact, you were like a *malach*! I, myself, testified to it!" In other words, the *satan* reminds us that we fail to achieve not because we can't achieve, but because we don't want to.

Shulchan Aruch Hilchos Yom Kippur ends with the *halachos* of building a *sukkah*. This is surprising, as *sukkah* does not seem to have anything to do with *Yom Kippur*. One explanation is that this placement reminds us to make sure to involve ourselves in *mitzvos* immediately after *Yom Kippur*, so that the *satan* won't have a chance to prosecute us.

But the truth is that the *satan* has an opportunity to accuse us even before we start planning to build the *sukkah*. The first thing we do upon returning home from *shul* after Yom Kippur is make *brachos* – the *brachos* of *havdalah*, as well as *brachos* on food. How much *kavanah* do we have when we make those *brachos*?

In the time of David HaMelech, there was a plague that killed one hundred people every day. *Chazal* tell us that in an effort to stop the plague, it was instituted that every individual recite one hundred *brachos* a day.[3] Making those *brachos* is what saved them. Saying *brachos* is clearly a *segulah* for life.

The reason that *brachos* have this power is that there is no better way to connect to Hashem than through *brachos*. Through them, a person can spend his entire day connecting to Hashem. When he gets up in the morning and drinks a cup a coffee, he makes two *brachos* – one before and one after. Throughout *Shacharis*, he says some more *brachos*, and when he eats breakfast, even more *brachos*. When he goes to *kollel* or to work, he has a snack, uses the bathroom, eats lunch, davens *Minchah*, and so on. These are all chances to make more

---

3. במדבר רבה פרשה י״ח כ״א

brachos and connect to Hashem! The *pasuk* tells us, "ואתם הדבקים בה' אלקיכם, חיים כלכם היום"[4] – those who connect to Hashem merit life. This is why *brachos* are a *segulah* for longevity. By making *brachos* all day, we are constantly connecting to Hashem!

At a later point in his life, Rav Shach took upon himself to always *bentch* from a *bentcher*. He once advised someone who came to him to take on the same *kabbalah*. A few years later, after Rav Shach had already passed away, that man went to see Rav Michel Yehuda Lefkowitz. He explained that he had heeded Rav Shach's instructions for many years, and he felt it was time to take upon himself something else, to grow in another area of Yiddishkeit. Having demonstrated his ability to keep a *kabbalah*, the man expected Rav Michel Yehuda to suggest something much more advanced for him to take on, but the Rav's response was not quite what he had anticipated. "Now," Rav Michel Yehuda told him, "take upon yourself to always say the *brachah* of *Asher Yatzar* with *kavanah*, and remember that *Asher Yatzar* is not *tefillas haderech*; don't walk around as you say it!"

We are now going to daven *Ne'ilah*, a *tefillah* that everyone davens with great *kavanah*. Let's hold on to the inspiration and later tonight let us make *brachos* with the proper *kavanah*. Once Yom Kippur ends and the *satan* is once again allowed to prosecute, he will try to do so as soon as he can. We have to make sure we don't give him that opportunity.

---

4. דברים ד:ד

It's Not To Late

During the *Aseres Yemei Teshuvah*, we are to look at ourselves as *beinonim* people in the middle who are תלויים ועומדים our judgment is hanging in the balance. As long as the verdict has not been declared, we can change it very easily. However, once it's settled, it's very difficult to change. as we near the end of the day it's a final chance to be written or get written in the sifrei tzadikim.

A story is told about a group of people who were unsuccessful at raising the funds necessary to build a new *shul* from scratch, the congregation's building committee settled on buying a pre-fab structure which would be delivered to the empty plot of land they had already purchased. Everyone came to watch the new *shul* being delivered. As the crane began to lower the building into place, four men were stationed around the spot where it was intended to go – one on each side – to make sure that the crane would position it directly on the foundation that had been laid for it.

As the structure got closer to the ground, the man on the south side yelled, "Three inches north!" The men pushed the building slightly to the left.

"Three inches west!" the man on the eastern side yelled, and they pushed.

"Too far! Move it half an inch back east!" called out the man on the western side.

When it was perfectly in position, the crane lowered the building to the ground, and the congregation subsequently moved into its new home.

Close to a year later, the people of the shul noticed that the building was slowly sinking. Upon investigating, it was discovered that it had actually been laid a couple of inches off the foundation. The building would have to be moved over, but how?

"Why don't we push it?" suggested one of the young children in the *shul*.

The *shul* members look at him quizzically.

"How would we push the building?" they asked him.

"What do you mean?" he responded. "Don't you all remember how, when the building was delivered, four men were able to move the building? We have many more people in the shul. If we all work together, it shouldn't be a big deal to push it a little bit."

"Son," one of the older members explained to him, "then, the building was being held up by a crane. When it's suspended in the air like that, it's easy to move. Once it's settled, moving it is next to impossible."

Now, as we begin *Ne'ilah*, the judgement is still hanging in the air. We can still move it where we want it to be. What we need is a commitment to hold on to the inspiration and to carry it with us throughout the year.

When we do our part, the *Ribono Shel Olam* will purify us and grant us a *gmar chasimah tovah*.

The Day that Lasts a Year

The *Sefer HaChinuch* explains that a *Kohen* is allowed to become *tamei* for his close relatives because, in essence, he is no different from the rest of the nation. Although there are certain times that he is busy with the *avodah* in the *Beis HaMikdash*, he is still fully connected to his relatives, as well as to benefiting from and enjoying this world. Since he is connected to his family members, he has an emotional need to become *tamei* for them, and therefore is permitted. In contrast, a *Kohen Gadol* and a *nazir* are called "*kadosh laHashem*," sanctified for Hashem; they are disconnected from any pleasures of this world so that they can always focus on the *nefesh*. Therefore, the Torah does not allow them to become *tamei* even for close relatives. They do not have the necessary connection to them and do not have that emotional need.[1]

---

1. ספר החינוך, מצוה שעו

The *Chinuch* notes that although the *Kohen Gadol*'s status is permanent, whereas the *nazir*'s status is temporary by nature, the same reasoning applies to the *nazir*. Although the *nazir* loses his official status with the completion of his *nezirus* period, he merits Heavenly assistance to further sanctify himself for the rest of his life. As *Chazal* teach us, הבא ליטהר מסייעין אותו.[2] When one comes to purify himself, Heaven will assist him. Through a single day* spent in a state of purity, one can merit to spend the rest of his days pure.

We can learn from here that the power of spending even just one day focused on spiritual growth can give a person the momentum to continue the process forever. If this is true of a *nazir*, who becomes holy by separating himself from wine and by refraining from cutting his hair, how much more so does it apply to us on Yom Kippur, when we spend the entire day abstaining from physicality, focusing instead on becoming holy and close to Hashem. This one day certainly has the power to help us spend the rest of our days in purity.

This idea of the *Chinuch* helped me gain a deeper understanding of a story that I had thought was nothing more than a *"Chassidishe mayseh"*:

> A Chassid from America had traveled to Antwerp to spend Yom Kippur with his Rebbe, Reb Yankele, the Pshevorsker Rebbe. After *Kol Nidrei*, he went to speak with Reb Yankele. "Let me tell you a story," the Rebbe told him. "A wealthy man promised his soon-to-be son-in-law that he would provide the new couple financial support for ten years. Ten days into their marriage, the new husband received a notice from his father-in-law that the time had come for him to begin looking for his own source of income, because he would no longer be supporting him. The bewildered son-in-law demanded

---

2. יומא לח:
*the chinuch writes one day although nazirus is 30 days

an explanation. 'Oh, I didn't forget my commitment,' his father-in-law assured him, 'but the *pasuk* says, יום לשנה,[3] a year for a day. Using that rule, you have already been married for ten years!' 'Well, in that case,' the quick-witted son-in-law responded, 'I ought to divorce your daughter. We've been married for ten years already, and we don't have any children!'"[4]

After finishing the story, the Rebbe moved on to the next person on line, leaving the American visitor very confused. Is this what I came to Antwerp for, he wondered to himself, for the Rebbe to tell me this strange story?

The visitor returned to his lodgings and sat down to learn a *sefer* on the topic of Yom Kippur. The *sefer* discussed the significance of mentioning the *Cheit HaMeraglim* on Yom Kippur. (Some of the *pesukim* in the Yom Kippur davening are from the *parshah* of the *Meraglim*, including the *pasuk*, "ויאמר ה' סלחתי כדברך.")

The reason for this, the *sefer* explained, is that immediately after Yom Kippur, the *satan* tries to prosecute us. "Look at *Klal Yisrael* now!" he says. "They don't seem to be on such a high level anymore."

"But look how they were on Yom Kippur," Hashem responds. "And *yom lashanah*, so it is counted as though they were this way for a whole year!"

---

3. This *pasuk* is found in the context of the story of the *Meraglim*. When they returned from spying in Eretz Yisroel, Hashem said that the Jews would have to spend forty years in the desert, יום לשנה, one year for each of the forty days the *Meraglim* spent in Eretz Yisroel.

4. See יבמות סד., where the *Gemara* rules that a couple that has been married for ten years and does not have any children should divorce.

"That makes no sense!" the *satan* retorts. "How can you count one day as an entire year?!"

"Many years ago," Hashem replies, "when I decreed that the Jews should spend forty years in the desert, *yom lashanah* for the forty days the *Meraglim* spent in Eretz Yisrael, you didn't have any complaints..."

The message the Rebbe was conveying to the visitor with the anecdote he told him was the same message he would later see in the *sefer* he was learning from: One day can have the power of an entire year. As the *Chinuch* explains, one can be so inspired from one day that the one day can end up changing his entire life. Let us utilize this day of Yom Kippur to inspire us.

Step By Step

We are coming to the close of Yom Kippur. "היום יפנה, השמש יבא ויפנה," "The day is taking leave, the sun is setting." "נבואה שעריך," "We approach your gates." We have one last chance. How can we get through the gates, the *shaarei teshuvah*?

Rav Chaim Aryeh Zev Ginsburg, Rav of Chafetz Chaim of Cedarhurst, related to me how he caught COVID-19 in March 2020. Gasping for breath, he was admitted to the hospital and put on a ventilator. After six and a half weeks, he returned home, very weak and unable to move his right leg due to severe nerve damage. He needed intensive physical therapy to learn to walk again. It was very difficult and painful, but he discovered inner strength that he never knew he had, and he managed to push through.

Many people ask him what motivated him to persevere the way that he did. He tells them how, many years ago, while visiting Eretz

Yisrael, he davened *Maariv* in a shul in Yerushalayim. It was the week of the *shloshim* of the Rosh Yeshiva of the Brisk Yeshiva of Chicago, Rav Ahron Soloveichik *zt"l*, and on the table in the *shul* was a booklet containing a brief biography of the Rosh Yeshivah. One of the stories told of a massive stroke that Rav Ahron had suffered, which left him confined to a wheelchair and with difficulty speaking. Regular therapy sessions were required to help him regain his former abilities, and a *talmid* of his would accompany him to each session. While accompanying Rav Ahron to one such session, one of the *talmidim* noticed that as he struggled to walk, Rav Ahron's lips were moving. Leaning in closer to hear what Rav Ahron was saying, the *talmid* heard, to his surprise, words from *Mussaf* of Yom Kippur. With each step he took, Rav Ahron would murmur the words the *Kohen Gadol* would say during the *avodah* of Yom Kippur: "אחת, אחת ואחת, אחת ושתים, אחת ושלש," "One, one and one, one and two, one and three..." As he took one step after another, the Rosh Yeshivah was performing his own form of *avodah*.

When Rabbi Ginsburg read the moving story, he wrote it down in his notes and filed it away. At that time, he didn't know why he had to be in that particular shul precisely the week that pamphlet was on the table. However, Hashem knew the challenge he would face years later, and, as Rabbi Ginsburg says, "He gave me the story that gave me the strength to climb back to myself. During the times when I felt like I couldn't exert my muscles any further, I would count, 'אחת, אחת ואחת...' Instead of feeling sorry for myself, I envisioned the grueling exercises as my personal *avodah*."

Each one of us has his or her own personal *avodah*, step by step – "אחת, אחת ואחת..." We can change who we are by making this *kabbalah* to move forward.

At times, we may fall, but just as Rav Ahron and Rabbi Ginsburg pushed themselves forward step-by-step, through hardships and setbacks – "אחת, אחת ואחת, אחת ושתים," until they made headway– we, too, must begin moving forward today in our *avodas Hashem,* step-by-step.

May we be *zocheh* to the fulfillment of the *Kohen Gadol*'s *tefillah* after he counted אחת ואחת: "אנא בשם, כפר נא לעוונות ולפשעים... ככתוב: כי ביום הזה יכפר עליכם לטהר אתכם מכל חטאותיכם לפני ה'."

Act on the Inspiration

After looking high and low for a suitable spouse for his only daughter, the king's search was finally up. He found the man whom he wished to take as his new son-in-law. The young gentleman and the princess got married and moved far away. The king missed his daughter terribly, and soon after the wedding, he made arrangements to visit and stay by her new home for several days. During his visit, he was delighted to see how well his new son-in-law cared for his daughter.

The night before his departure, as he packed his belongings, the king's daughter came to his room, her eyes filled with tears. "Please!" she begged her father, "don't leave me here! Take me home! My husband is abusing me, and I'm suffering so much!"

"I don't understand," the king said to her, puzzled. "I watched him the whole time I was here. I saw how kindly he speaks to you and how nicely he treats you."

"No," his daughter responded, shaking her head sadly. "He was just putting on a show for you. As soon as you leave, he will go right back to his old ways!"

Hashem sends each of us down to this world with a pure *neshamah* and instructs the *guf* to take good care of it and keep it pristine. But people often focus on the *guf* too much and end up abusing the *neshamah*. During the *Aseres Yemei Teshuvah*, Hashem comes to "visit us" to see how we are treating the *neshamos* He gave us. During His visit, we *daven* more seriously, give more *tzedakah*, and take upon ourselves extra *chumros*. But are we just putting on a show? When we blow the *shofar* at the end of *Ne'ilah*, the signal of the *Shechinah*'s "departure," we should remember not to go right back to our old ways.

We must hold on to today's inspiration. The *pasuk* in *Acharei Mos* instructs, "ופשט את בגדי הבד... ורחץ את בשרו במים," "He shall remove the linen garments... then he shall wash himself with water."[1] The Chasam Sofer questions why the *Kohen Gadol* immerses himself when changing from the white linen garments into to the golden garments.[2] After all, immersing makes sense when one is rising in *kedushah*, not when descending. The white garments, which the *Kohen Gadol* wore upon entering the *Kodesh HaKodoshim*, had a higher level of *kedushah* than the golden garments. Why did he immerse before changing into the garments of a lower state?

The Chasam Sofer explains that when a person sanctifies himself and gains additional *kedushah*, all the *mitzvos* he performs afterwards are on a higher level. The *Kohen Gadol*, having performed the *avodah* in the *Kodesh HaKodoshim* wearing the white garments, reached a higher level of *kedushah*, and everything he did from then on was on a higher plane. Thus, when he donned the golden garments after performing the *avodah* in the *Kodesh HaKodoshim*, he had added

---

1. ויקרא טז:כג-כד

2. תורת משה פרשת אחרי מות, ויקרא טז:כג

kedushah, and he therefore needed to immerse himself, since he was entering a higher level.

Similarly, when one moves on from Yom Kippur after forty days of *avodah*, starting from Rosh Chodesh Elul, he should take the new levels he has attained and use them to add more *kedushah* to every *mitzvah* he will do.

Take Action

Under the rule of the Communist regime of the Soviet Union, learning Torah was a serious offense, punishable by forced labor in Siberia. One *rav* courageously risked his life to regularly deliver clandestine *shiurim*. One day, he decided that he would like to have an audience with the refuseniks, who were not particularly interested in learning Torah, to try to inspire them to change their ways. The refuseniks agreed to meet with the *rav*, and they gathered secretly in a basement. The *rav* began to speak, and surprisingly, the refuseniks were very moved by his inspiring words. All of a sudden, a loud knock was heard at the door. Fearing the worst, one of the attendees grabbed the *sefarim* and stashed them out of sight, another found a laundry basket and hid under the clothing, others climbed out the window, and the remaining few pulled out a pack of cards. By the time the KGB agents barged in, all they saw was a small group of people playing cards. The *rav*'s speech was definitely over.

Several weeks later, the Rav reached out to the refuseniks and asked if they would be interested in reconvening. They were a little puzzled. What had the *rav* not accomplished last time that he felt he could do in a second meeting?

"When I was speaking to you last time," the *rav* explained to them, "I felt that you were all indeed inspired by the words you heard. Some of you had tears in your eyes; I even heard some sobbing. But the 'inspiration' you got from the KGB was much greater; when they came, you all got 'inspired' and immediately sprang into action. Without action, inspiration alone is worthless."

As we reach the end of Yom Kippur, we must keep this lesson in mind. No matter how inspired we are, the inspiration is useless if we neglect to put it into action. We have to take some practical change with us.

Limud Zechus

Rav Levi Yitzchak of Berditchev is famous for constantly being *melamed zechus* on fellow Jews. It is said that he once saw a Jew smoking on Yom Kippur.

"Do you know that today is Yom Kippur?" Rav Levi Yitzchak asked him gently.

"Yes, I know," the man replied.

"Do you know that *Yidden* go to shul on Yom Kippur?" the Rav asked.

"Yes, I know," the man replied again.

"Do you know that one is not allowed to smoke on Yom Kippur?" the Rav asked, again receiving an affirmative response.

"*Ribono Shel Olam*!" Rav Levi Yitzchok proclaimed, looking up to Heaven. "Look at your righteous children! This man could have lied three times, but he insisted on telling the truth!"

Another Yom Kippur story told about Rav Levi Yitzchak took place after *Maariv* on Yom Kippur night. Addressing those that had come to *daven*, the Berditchever told them that according to Halachah, since one is not allowed to utter Hashem's name in vain, one may not say a *brachah* if there is the slightest possibility that it won't be valid, as he might be saying Hashem's name in vain. "Tonight," Rav Levi Yitzchak continued, "during *Shmoneh Esrei*, every member of *Klal Yisrael* said the *brachah*, "ברוך... מלך מוחל וסולח לעוונתינו ולעוונות עמו בית ישראל...," blessing "the King who forgoes and forgives our transgression and the transgressions of His nation, Yisrael."

"*Ribono shel Olam!*" Rav Levi Yitzchok cried, raising his eyes Heavenward. "You cannot cause your children to violate the tremendous *issur* of reciting an invalid *brachah*! You have no choice but to forgive them!"

These stories were not the kind we would hear in *yeshivah* during the *Yomim Nora'im*; these are, after all, "*Chassidishe maysehs*." On *Kol Nidrei* night, we expected to hear fiery speeches filled with intense *mussar*. A story I recently heard, however, taught me that this wasn't always the case.

> The Chofetz Chaim was addressing his *yeshiva* after *Kol Nidrei*. "We just recited the *pasuk,* "ונסלח לכל עדת בני ישראל ולגר הגר בתוכם, כי לכל העם בשגגה," "The entire Jewish nation will be forgiven, as well as the convert who lives among them, for all the people acted unintentionally."[1]
> "Imagine," he continued, "an old non-Jewish man decides to convert, and he accepts the Torah and *mitzvos*. Shortly after his conversion, he makes a mistake and does an *aveirah*. Would we hold him accountable? Of course not. What does he know? How much has he learned already? When did he have a chance to get used to doing *mitzvos*, to stand up to *nisyonos*? Even though

---

1. במדבר טו:כו

he is a full-fledged Jew, our expectations of him are limited."

The Chafetz Chaim began to cry as he continued. "And all of us, what do we know? How much have we learned? What can really be expected from us?! We implore Hashem: 'ונסלח לכל עדת בני ישראל,' 'Forgive all of *Klal Yisrael*,' in the same way that you forgive 'הגר הגר בתוכם,' 'the convert who lives among them,' because 'לכל העם בשגגה,' 'the entire nation acted unintentionally.'

Reb Yoel Kaflut, a *talmid* of the Chafetz Chaim, explained that at this auspicious time between *Kol Nidrei* and *Maariv* on Yom Kippur, the Chafetz Chaim would not speak *divrei hisorerus*. He felt it was more important to spend this time being *melamed zechus* on everyone. As the Chafetz Chaim himself writes in the *sefer Shem Olam*, one who is *melamed zechus* on *Klal Yisrael* is treated by Hashem *middah keneged middah*, and the angels will be *melamed zechus* on him in the Heavenly Court.

We live in a weak generation, in which people become upset with their behavior and give up easily. I would therefore like to follow in the footsteps of both the Chafetz Chaim and the Berditchever Rebbe and take this opportunity to be *melamed zechus* on *Klal Yisrael*.

A *rav* was once approached by a brokenhearted man, who bemoaned how every year, he was very inspired when saying *Aleinu* on the *Yamim Nora'im*. He felt as though he had reached great heights and found the words so powerful and meaningful. "This year," he told the Rav, "as I was experiencing that special feeling, when I reached the words, 'לתקן עולם במלכות שד-י,' I had a rude awakening. Reality hit me. Every day of the year, I say *Aleinu* three times. Many of those times, I simply mumble the words as fast as I can. I'm often jingling my car keys, slowly making my way out of *shul*. Now, I feel like a faker. I realized that on Rosh Hashanah and Yom Kippur, when I have that special feeling, I'm really just following the crowd, getting caught up in the moment."

This man's realization is reminiscent of a famous story about the Satmar Rebbe:

> While entertaining the crowd at a *mitzvah tantz*, the *badchan* asked the Satmar Rebbe permission to imitate the Rebbe's davening on the *Yomim Nora'im*. The Rebbe gave his consent, and the *badchan* began performing a spectacular impression of the Rebbe, with all the nuances, in the Rebbe's high-pitched voice, intermittently sobbing, as the crowd roared with laughter. The *badchan* continued until he noticed that the Rebbe was in tears. He immediately stopped and ran over to the Rebbe to beg forgiveness.
>
> "You didn't do anything wrong!" the Rebbe assured him. "I am crying because when I saw how well you imitated me, I thought to myself that perhaps when I am davening, I am simply imitating myself!"

The man who experienced special inspiration during *Aleinu* felt the same way. It was as though the instructions in the Artscroll *machzor* read, "Cry here."

"Let me ask you a question," his *rav* said to him. "If you were captured by a bunch of terrorists, and they put a gun to your head and said, 'Either bow to this idol or be killed,' would you bow?"

"Of course not," the man replied. "*Avodah zarah* is a יהרג ואל יעבור. One must give up his life rather than transgress!"

"I thought so," said the Rav. "Now, that means that every day, at every moment, you're willing to sacrifice your life for *kevod Shamayim*. So when are you expressing your true self? When you say *Aleinu* slowly, with special feeling, during the *Yomim Nora'im*, or when you speed through it in the middle of your work day? Which one is the real you? Clearly, the one during the year is fake, and your *Yomim Nora'im* self is real!". We shouldn't despair but we must do the best we can.

Deep Down

There is a problem I have felt in the past while reciting *Viduy*, and I am sure that I am not alone. As I *klap al cheit*, I feel remorseful for all my *aveiros*. But then, I start getting overwhelmed when I realize that I went through the exact same thing last year, and the year before as well. Did I fix everything then? "על חטא שחטאנו לפניך בלשון הרע." Have I perfected my speech? "במאכל ובמשתה." Did I have *kavana* when I said *brachos*? Did I feel a real sense of *hakaros hatov* each time I ate? "זלזול הורים ומורים." Am I doing more *kibbud eim*, calling more, visiting more? I could go on and on. At times, I've felt I should just give up. I'm a failure, a lost cause.

But then something occurred to me while reciting the *tefillah* לא-ל עורך דין. In that *tefillah*, we refer to Hashem as the "בוחן לבבות ביום דין," the One who inspects hearts on the Day of Judgment. These words should create tremendous fear, when we realize that Hashem is looking into our hearts. The *tefillah* continues, however: "לגולה עמוקות בדין," "To the One who reveals the depths in the judgment." Hashem looks into the depths of our hearts, into who we really are. Who is the real you? Deep down, we all want to improve, and Hashem knows that. This is very comforting, and it leads to that which we say several stanzas later: "לכובש כעסו בדין," "To the One who suppresses His anger in the judgement." His knowledge of our true desire pacifies Hashem's anger.

The Rambam mentions this concept in a famous *halachah* in *Hilchos Geirushin*.[1] The Rambam rules that although a *get* given by a man who was forced to do so is generally invalid, nevertheless, if the man was forced by *Beis Din*, it is valid. The reason, the Rambam explains, is that deep down, every Jew wants to do the right thing, but his *yetzer hara* gets in the way. When *Beis Din* forces him and he says, "רוצה אני," "I want," even if his *yetzer hara* tells him that he really **doesn't** want, deep down, in his soul, he does, and it is not considered a forced *get*.

In a similar vein, *Chazal* tell us that even *resha'im* are "מלאים מצות כרמון," full of *mitzvos* like a pomegranate. Even the word רשע is "רע" only on the outside; inside is the ש, שד-י, the נשמת אדם, נר אלוקים.

> Allowed to take only one suitcase of clothing and no valuables, a man leaving the Soviet Union to the United States presented his solitary piece of luggage to the KGB for inspection. In addition to the man's clothing, they found a bust of Lenin's head, and they demanded an explanation. "I have to leave the Soviet Union," the man explained, "but I never want to forget the great leader of our motherland, and I want to show my children and grandchildren what he looked like." They gave him permission to take it.

---

1. הלכות גרושין ב:כ.

When he arrived in the United States, the customs officials similarly demanded an explanation for the sculpture. "Are you trying to bring Communism here?" they asked him accusingly. "No," he explained. "This evil man destroyed my country, my religion, and my family. I never want to forget what he did to me, and I want to show my children and grandchildren how he looked, so that they, too, will never forget." "Fine," they said. "You may keep it."

When the man arrived at his new home, a third explanation was demanded of him, this time by his family. "Why did you bring this head of Lenin?" they asked him. "Well," he told them proudly, "on the surface, you see Lenin's head. Underneath it, however, is actually eight pounds of gold that I managed to smuggle out of the Soviet Union!"

On the outside, we may look like a Lenin, but if we remove our outer, superficial layers, we will discover the gold, the "real me" that's inside. It is because of these *middos*, which we inherited from our ancestors, that Hashem loves us so much. Even though we sometimes fail, deep down, in our DNA, there's purity and goodness.

Unconditional Love

In the *parshah* of *Matan Torah*, the *pasuk* describes, "ואשא אתכם על כנפי נשרים," "I carried you on eagles' wings." The Chasam Sofer poses an interesting question: The *Gemara* tells us that there are four features a bird must possess to be considered a kosher species. If even one of the signs is missing, the species is rendered impure. The eagle is missing all four. Why, asks the Chasam Sofer, did Hashem carry us on the wings of eagles, the most impure of all birds? Wouldn't it make more sense to carry us on a dove, a kosher species, a bird that *Klal Yisrael* themselves are compared to? The reason Hashem chose the eagle, the Chasam Sofer explains, was to teach us that even if we were to have every type of impurity possible, Hashem still loves us. Hashem sees the goodness deep down inside us. "אלוקי, נשמה שנתת בי טהורה היא," "My G-d, the soul that you placed in me is pure."

Over the course of the twenty-five hours of Yom Kippur, we repeat the thirteen *Middos HaRachamim* multiple times. One of those *middos* is אמת, truth. What does truth have to do with mercy? אמת means that Hashem doesn't look at us the way we think we are, but instead looks at us with "truth" – at who we really are, deep down, despite all our frailties, faults, flaws and failings. When He judges us, He takes the whole picture into account.

Nonetheless, we must l do our part and finds ways to improve and show Hashem that we really mean it. This is why taking on a *kabbalah* is so powerful. The *kabbalah* is not what tips the scale. It is not what causes us to have a good year. Rather, the *kabbalah* is a display of who we really are, what our essence is and where we are heading.

Rav Yisroel Salanter once gave a *mashal*, which I will update for today's times, about a man who boarded a bus in Yerushalayim, intending to go to Bnei Brak. He had been told that the trip would take an hour. Two hours passed, and he still had yet to hear an announcement for his destination. "Why is it taking so long to reach Bnei Brak?" he asked the passenger next to him. "Bnei Brak?" the passenger said. "This bus is headed south, traveling farther away from Bnei Brak. To get to Bnei Brak, you need to be on a bus traveling north." Realizing his mistake, the man got off the bus at the next stop and hopped onto a north-bound bus. At that moment, said Rav Yisroel, even though he was two hours away from Bnei Brak, he was better off than he had been when he was on the previous bus leaving Yerushalayim and only one hour away. Now, he was at least heading in the right direction.

As long as we are heading in the right direction, Hashem will overlook our faults and accept our *teshuvah*, and this year, *im yirtzeh Hashem*, we will be carried על כנפי נשרים to the בימינו במהרה שלימה גאולה.

Partial *Taharah*

The *mishnah* teaches:

אמר רבי עקיבא: אשריכם ישראל, לפני מי אתם מטהרין, מי מטהר אתכם? אביכם שבשמים, שנאמר, (יחזקאל ל"ו) "וזרקתי עליכם מים טהורים וטהרתם", ואומר, (ירמיה י"ז) "מקוה ישראל ה'", מה מקוה מטהר את הטמאים, אף הקדוש ברוך הוא מטהר את ישראל.

    Rabbi Akiva said: Yisrael, you are fortunate! Before whom do you become purified, and who purifies you? Your Father in Heaven, as the *pasuk* states, "I will sprinkle pure water onto you, and you will be purified, and the *pasuk* states, "Hashem is the *mikveh* of Yisrael." Just as a *mikveh* purifies those who are *tamei*, so does Hashem purify Yisrael.[1]

    Why does the *mishnah* specifically mention that the *mikveh*

---

1. יומא ח:ט

purifies "those who are *tamei*?" Who else needs to be purified? The *mishnah* could have simply said, "מה המקוה מטהר," "Just as the *mikveh* purifies."

This can be explained by examining an interesting *halachah* pertaining to a person in the midst of the seven-day procedure required to be purified from *tumas meis* (in the time of the *Beis HaMikdash*). In this process, the person becoming *tahor* is sprinkled with the ashes of the *parah adumah* on the third and seventh days. The purification from *tumas sheretz*, on the other hand, is only one day; the one who was *tamei* becomes *tahor* at nightfall of the day he immerses in the *mikveh*. What happens if someone in the middle of the seven-day procedure for *tumas meis* becomes *tamei* from a *sheretz* on the fourth day? It would seem that there wouldn't be any point in going to the *mikveh* then, as he won't be completely *tahor* anyway until the end of the seven-day process. However, the *halachah* is that he must purify himself and rid himself of the *tumas sheretz* as soon as possible. Even a partial *taharah* counts.

This is why Rabbi Akiva specifies that Hashem purifies us just as a *mikveh* "purifies those who are *tamei*." The same way that a *mikveh* can grant a person who is *tamei* partial purification, even though he still will not be completely *tahor*, Hashem purifies Yisrael, even though we remain partially *tamei*, having so much more to do. When we do *teshuvah* and try to improve ourselves a little bit, Hashem could simply send us away and tell us to come back when we're completely *tahor*. Instead, Hashem accepts even the small amount that we can do, as long as we do something – a partial *taharah*. As *Chazal* teach us, "אמר הקדוש ברוך הוא לישראל, בני, פתחו לי פתח אחד של תשובה כחודה של מחט, ואני פותח לכם פתחים שיהיו עגלות וקרניות נכנסות בו," "Hashem says to Yisrael: My children, open an entrance of *teshuvah* for me like the point of a needle, and I will open for you an entrance that wagons and chariots can pass through."[2]

---

2. שיר השירים רבה ה:ב. The Kotzker Rebbe explains that the analogy is to a needle because although it has a small hole, that hole goes all the way through.

Shas begins with the words, "מאימתי קורין את שמע בערבית," "From when can we read *Shema* in the evening?" In addition to the simple meaning, we can explain this question allegorically. The *mishnah* is asking: How can one be *mekabel ol Malchus Shamayim* in the "evening," when it looks dark, when one is depressed and feels unaccomplished? We often ask ourselves this question. Yom Kippur arrives after a forty-day *avodah* of self-improvement, and what do we have to show for it? As we say in the *Viduy* of *Ne'ilah*, "מה אנו, מה חיינו," "What are we [worth], what is our life [worth]?" Answers the *mishnah*, "משעה שהכהנים נכנסים לאכול בתרומתם," "From the time that the *Kohanim* [who were *tamei* are able to] enter to eat their *terumah*." When nightfall arrives on the day he immersed in the *mikveh*, a *Kohen* who was *tamei* can eat *terumah* again. Even though this *Kohen* very often cannot eat *kodshim* until he brings certain *korbanos* the next day, he can eat *terumah* at nightfall, because he has received a partial *taharah*. This *mishnah* is telling us that it's not "all or nothing." As long as you have done as much as you can, you will be purified. All we need to do is begin the journey toward *taharah*, toward complete *teshuvah*.

"ואנחנו כורעים....," the *chazan* on Yom Kippur chanted as he dropped to his knees. Standing by his side was the eldest of his five sons, ready to help his father stand up when he finished bowing. This son had stood at his father's side every Yom Kippur for many years. When he got married and moved out of town, the next son assumed the position, and the next two brothers followed suit. Eventually, the fourth brother got married and moved out of town. The following Yom Kippur, the *chazan* went up to the *amud* alone. The youngest son had gone "off the *derech*," and *shul* was generally not a place he could be found.

Suddenly, when the *chazan* reached *Aleinu*, the door of the *shul* opened. Sporting a ponytail and covered in tattoos, the *chazan*'s youngest son walked in and made his way to the front of the *shul* to stand next to his father. As the *chazan* finished bowing, the son extended his hand to help his father up, but the *chazan* pushed him away. The same thing happened year after year, for many years.

After the *chazan* passed away, all the sons were sitting *shivah* together. One of the members of the *shul* came to visit, and he asked the youngest son the question that was bothering everyone: Why did he keep coming back to *shul* each Yom Kippur if it was clear from the way his father pushed him away that he wasn't interested in his help? "You only saw him pushing me away," the son answered. "However, before he pushed me away, he would first pull me closer towards him, demonstrating how he still loved me. It was worth coming every year just for that."

There is no time of year that Hashem is "pulling us closer" more than at *Ne'ilah* on Yom Kippur. As we say in the special *Viduy* of *Ne'ilah*, "אתה נותן יד לפושעים," "You extend a hand to [accept] sinners." Had this *chazan's* son made the slightest move in the right direction, his father wouldn't have pushed him away. All we must do is the partial *teshuvah* we are able to do, and Hashem will pull us close to Him and keep us there.

A New "You"

Every year, before *Maariv* on Yom Kippur night, we say *Kol Nidrei*. I can't say that we *daven Kol Nidrei*, because it's not a *tefillah*; it's *hataras nedarim*. Indeed, upon reflection, it seems rather strange that we begin the holiest day of the year this way.

I once heard an interesting explanation for why this is our introduction to Yom Kippur. Before Rosh Hashanah, we take care of *aveiros bein adam laMakom*, and during *Aseres Yemei Teshuvah*, we take care of *aveiros bein adam lachaveiro*, for which Yom Kippur alone will not be *mechaper*. However, there is still one more area to work on – *bein adam l'atzmo*, man's responsibility to himself. A *neder* is a commitment, the responsibility one has to keep his word. But a *neder* is also the obligation one has to himself, what is expected of him based on his talents, strengths, and capabilities.

In order to live up to ourselves, however, we must first define who we really are.

In the *Kedushah* of Yom Kippur *Mussaf*, the *Ba'alei Kabbalah* inserted three different *tefillos* that one can say as the *chazan* says the word "איה." One is a request for *parnassah*, another for *ruach hakodesh*, and the third for good children. Why would anyone, especially on Yom Kippur, choose to *daven* for *parnassah* over *ruach hakodesh* or good children? It doesn't seem much of a choice. The answer given is that there is no real suggestion to choose the *tefillah* for *parnassah*; it's only there to give us an opportunity to choose *ruchniyus* over *gashmiyus*, to demonstrate who we really are and what's really important to us.

The early years of Moshe Rabbeinu's life were spent growing up as an adopted prince in Pharaoh's palace. The Torah tells us that he once went out to see the suffering of his fellow Jews. Noticing an Egyptian man hitting a Jew, the *pasuk* says, "ויפן כה וכה," "he turned this way and that."[1] On the simple level, this means that Moshe looked both ways to make sure no one was watching as he proceeded to kill the Egyptian. Rav Meir Shapiro *zt"l* suggested another explanation: In self-introspection, Moshe looked at both of his sides. Am I an Egyptian, having grown up in Pharaoh's palace? Or am I a Jew, having been born to Amram, the leader of the generation? Where do my loyalties lie? The *pasuk* continues, "וירא כי אין איש," "He saw there was no man." Moshe realized that with divided loyalties, you can't be a mensch; you can't be successful. He had to define himself. "ויך את המצרי," "He hit the Egyptian." Moshe uprooted the Egyptian part of himself and became Moshe Rabbeinu, the leader of *Klal Yisrael*.

We must follow Moshe's lead. We must uproot hopelessness and laziness – in other words, the *yetzer hara* – and discover who we really are so that we can fulfill our full potential.

Sometimes, we forget who we really are:

> Caught in a heavy snowstorm, the weary traveler

---

1. שמות ב:יב.

breathed a sigh of relief as he reached a small inn. However, to his dismay, the innkeeper informed him that all the rooms were taken. "What should I do?" the despondent traveler moaned. "I can't go back out in this snow!" Suddenly, the innkeeper thought of an idea. "You know what?" he told the traveler. "There's one room that has an extra bed. There's a clown staying there, and I'm sure he wouldn't mind having a roommate for the night." The clown consented, and the traveler made his way to the room, arranging with the innkeeper to wake him at 5:00 a.m. At five the next morning, when the sun had yet to rise, the traveler got dressed quietly, so as not to wake the clown, who was still sleeping, and left the inn to continue his journey. As dawn broke and the sun lit up the day, he noticed that people he passed were looking at him strangely, some quietly laughing. He couldn't understand why. Eventually, he passed a shop with large windows and caught a glimpse of his reflection, which quickly explained why people were so amused. He was wearing a clown's outfit. "Oy!" he said to himself. "The innkeeper made a mistake! He woke up the clown instead of me!"

Returning Home

Visitors to the *shul* in Moscow may notice that the *paroches* was dedicated by the former Rav, Rav Pinchas Goldschmidt, *l'ilui nishmas* Rav Shmarya Yehuda Leib Medalia. Rav Medalia became chief Rabbi of Moscow in 1933, during the Stalin era, and he worked tirelessly to raise the level of Yiddishkeit in Russia. Threats of persecution were constant. In October 1938, Pravda, the Soviet newspaper, printed stories about Rav Medalia being a foreign agent involved in anti-Soviet activity.

One year, as Yom Kippur was approaching, Stalin made it clear that no one was to take off work that day. The entire Yom Kippur, the *shul* remained empty, other than a few old people who couldn't work. Then, close to nightfall, as the work day ended, people started pouring in.

The Rav got up before a packed audience to speak before *Ne'ilah*.

He began with a story of two farmers who lived across the street from each other. One day, a chicken was found standing in the middle of the road. One farmer quickly grabbed it, claiming it belonged to him. The other farmer objected, insisting it was his.

Seeing that his protests were in vain, the second farmer proposed that they go to ask the wise man. The other farmer agreed, and the two accepted that they would listen to whatever the wise man said. The wise man heard them out, and, turning to the farmer holding the chicken, he instructed that it be placed back in the middle of the road. "If you want to know where it belongs," he said, "watch where it goes at the end of the day."

When the Rav finished his story, he looked at the people in the *shul*, most of whom had been working all Yom Kippur day and had come to *shul* just for *Ne'ilah*. He repeated the words of the wise man. "Place the chicken in the middle of the road; it won't stay there. If you want to know where it belongs, wait until the end of the day and it will return home." With those words, he ended his *drashah*. The next day, Rav Medalia was taken from his home and was never heard from again.

All year, people struggle in their *avodas Hashem*, but, on Yom Kippur, we are cut off from all physicality and spend twenty-five hours totally focused on the Creator of the World. This is the day we all come home.

You Can Do It

As we say *Viduy* and think about our shortcomings, we often feel that we're inadequate and it's too difficult to change, despite our desire to. When we think these thoughts, we should remember the *pasuk*, "כי קרוב אליך הדבר מאד, בפיך ובלבבך לעשותו", "For the matter is very close to you, in your mouth and in your heart, to do it."[1] The Ramban explains that this *pasuk* refers to *teshuvah*.

If *teshuvah* is close to us, why do we feel that it is so distant? I heard from Rav Avrohom Schorr that even though *teshuvah* is close to us, we are distant from ourselves. We don't know who we really are. We have so much untapped potential, and we don't even realize it, to the point that we believe that *teshuvah* is impossible. That's why the Torah tells us, "לא בשמים היא לאמר מי יעלה לנו השמימה ויקחה לנו", "It

---

1. דברים ל:יד.

is not in the heavens, that we would say, 'Who will go up for us to the heavens and get it for us?'"[2] Rashi on that *pasuk* quotes the *Gemara*: "שאלו היתה בשמים היית צריך לעלות אחריה וללומדה, "Because if it were in the heavens, you would have to go up after it and learn it."[3] The *Gemara* doesn't mean that we would have to physically go up to *Shamayim*. It means that there are times that it feels like things are so difficult for us, it is as if achievement is in *Shamayim*. Nevertheless, we are required to go after it, to do everything in our power to accomplish. When we do that, Hashem will give us the *siyata d'shmaya* to succeed.

For the last forty days, we have been saying the 27th *perek* of *Tehillim*, "לדוד, ה' אורי וישעי," after *davening*. The third *pasuk* reads, "אם תחנה עלי מחנה לא יירא לבי, אם תקום עלי מלחמה, בזאת אני בוטח," "If an army camps on me, my heart will not fear; if war rises up against me, I trust in this." What is "this," the "זאת" in which we trust? I once heard a very powerful explanation. Dovid Hamelech is saying: If I have "wars," meaning *nisyonos*, בזאת אני בוטח – I have faith in the knowledge that Hashem gave these *nisyonos* to me. I know I have the ability to overcome them, because if not, He wouldn't have given them to me. Hashem doesn't give us any test that we can't overcome.

A visitor to the Beis Yisrael was asked by the Rebbe which *yeshivah* he had learned in. "I learned in Ohr Someach," he replied, quickly adding, "But I'm not a *ba'al teshuvah*." "Why not?" the Rebbe asked him.

For forty days, we have been preparing for Yom Kippur. By now, we should have done *teshuvah*. If we haven't, we must ask ourselves: Why not?

One reason is that we live in a society in which everything comes easily. We don't have to go to the river to wash our clothing, we don't have to chop firewood to have heat, and we don't have to draw water

---

2. דברים ל:יב.

3. עירובין נה.

from a well. Daily life has been getting easier and easier in each generation. There are very few areas today in which a person has to put in real effort.

In fact, that's why *segulos* are so popular today; everyone is looking for a "quick fix." This has given a new meaning to the term "*Am Segulah*"...[4] *Chazal* ask, "מה יעשה אדם וינצל מחבלי של משיח," "What can a person do to be saved from the birth pangs of Mashiach?"[5] We hope the answer will be, "Give money to Kupat Ha'Ir," or, "Forty women should bake *challah* together." It's very disappointing when we see that the actual answer is, "יעסוק בתורה ובגמילות חסדים," "He should busy himself with Torah and doing *chesed*." There are no shortcuts.

Similarly, in our *avodah* of *teshuvah*, there's no easy way out.

On Yom Kippur, we cut ourselves off from all *inyanei Olam Hazeh*, from all *gashmiyus*, and we focus completely on *ruchniyus*. It's a day to contemplate who we really are, to think about what Hashem expects from us.

In *Sha'arei Teshuvah*, Rabbeinu Yonah notes, "אם האדם לא עורר נפשו מה יועילוהו המוסרים?" "If a person doesn't awaken himself, what will all the *mussar* do for him?"[6] If I don't make the effort to arouse myself, I won't be able to get started.

According to one explanation, we don't recite the *brachah* of *Shehechiyanu* at a *bris milah* because of the pain the child is experiencing.[7] If that is the case, why do we make a *Shehechiyanu* on Yom Kippur, when we're trembling in fear? I heard a fascinating insight to explain this. The *Shehechiyanu* on Yom Kippur is not recited over the day itself; rather, it's being recited upon becoming a new "you." As the Rambam writes, when a person does *teshuvah*, he

---

4. Literally, a treasured nation.
5. ילקוט שמעוני ירמיהו, רמז שי
6. שערי תשובה, שער שני אות כו
7. עי' בית יוסף יורה דעה סימן רסה

becomes "איש אחר," "A different man."[8] Yom Kippur is the day we start afresh, with a clean slate, the day we can plan in which area we will push ourselves to improve.

With this mindset, we will *im yirtzeh Hashem* be *zocheh* to a *gmar chasimah tovah*.

---

8. הלכות יסודי התורה פרק ז הלכה א

Embarrassed from *Cheit*

The year was 1942. In the Lodz Getto sat the Rebbe of Radeshitz, his spirits very down. It was the night before Yom Kippur, and the Nazis had cemented the entrances to all the *mikvaos*, claiming they were unsanitary. The Rebbe was deeply anguished; he desperately wanted to immerse himself in a *mikveh*, as he had always done. How could he go into Yom Kippur without a *tevilah*?

In the middle of the night, there was a knock at the Rebbe's door. Standing in the doorway was a teenage boy who had risked his life and broke the curfew to let the Rebbe know that a *mikveh* was available. In a house adjacent to the *mikveh*, the Jews in the ghetto had managed, using pen knives, spoons, and screw drivers, to create a small hole leading into the *mikveh*. The boy told the Rebbe that it was a secret, and only the *Rabbanim* in the ghetto were being told about it. Elated, the Rebbe took his *gabbai* with him, and, risking their lives, they made their way to the house where the entrance was. When they arrived, they went downstairs, holding a candle, and the Rebbe was amazed at what he saw: Hundreds of *Yidden* were cramped into a small basement, and, one by one, they were being hoisted up into the hole in the wall, immersing in the *mikveh*, and then being helped back out. The "secret" had obviously gotten out. (As we know, a "secret" by Yidden means telling only one person at a time...)

These people were living in the darkest moments of their lives. They had lost everything. Yet, all they were interested in was an opening for something pure, for *taharah*. Despite all the suffering, hardship, and starvation they were experiencing, with all the worries they had, first and foremost on their minds was purity, and they were willing to risk their lives for it.

Fortunately, we don't live under those conditions, but we are also in desperate need of *taharah*. Yom Kippur is the day to attain that *taharah*, as the *pasuk* tells us, "כי ביום הזה יכפר עליכם לטהר אתכם מכל חטאתיכם לפני ה' תטהרו," "On this day He will cleanse you, to purify you from all your sins; in front of Hashem, you will be purified."[1] Today, *HaKadosh Baruch Hu* Himself is the *mikveh*, as the last *mishnah* in *Maseches Yoma* famously concludes: "אף מה מקוה מטהר את הטמאים, הקדוש ברוך הוא מטהר את ישראל," "Just as a *mikveh* purifies the impure, so does *HaKadosh Baruch Hu* purify Yisrael." The *mishnah* learns this from the *pasuk* in *Yirmiyah*: "מקוה ישראל ה'."[2] The comparison of Hashem's cleansing of us to a *mikveh* implies that Hashem not only forgives us, but also purifies us from any *tumah*, any scar or residue left over from the *aveirah*. We become spotless.

However, notes the Zhelemer Rav, not everything that is *tamei* can be purified in a *mikveh*. A *kli cheres*, an earthenware item, can

---

1. ויקרא טז:ל.

2. יז:יג.

only become *tahor* by breaking it. As we stand here now, in desperate need of forgiveness and a clean slate, we are composed of two parts: a pure *neshamah* and a *guf* made from *afar min ha'adamah,* dirt of the ground.³ Our task is to make sure that our *neshamah* dominates the *guf* and not vice-versa. Our focus should be on Torah and *mitzvos,* not on materialism. Then, we will be defined as "*neshamah Yidden,*" and the *mikveh* can purify us. But if we let the *gashmiyus* dominate, if the *afar min ha'adamah* leads the way, we become like a *kli cheres,* and the *mikveh* won't be able to purify us.

Nonetheless, there is an *eitzah* even for those in the category of *kli cheres.* The *pasuk* in *Tehillim* says: "לב נשבר ונדכה אלקים לא תבזה," "A broken and destitute heart, You, *Elokim,* won't despise."⁴ Even when Hashem is acting as "*Elokim,*" the name that reflects *middas hadin,* He will never reject a person who possesses a broken and humble heart. If we are truly ashamed of the way we have lived – even if, at the moment, we are in the *kli cheres* category – we can still become *tahor.*

The *Shaarei Teshuvah* writes that feeling shame is an integral part of *teshuvah.*⁵ Interestingly, the word תשובה includes the letters that spell the word בושה, shame, demonstrating its importance as part of the *teshuvah* process.

Chazal teach us: "כל העושה דבר עבירה ומתבייש בו מוחלין לו על כל עונותיו," "Anyone who does an *aveirah* and is ashamed from it, all his sins are forgiven."⁶ This is derived from the story of Shaul reviving the spirt of Shmuel HaNavi to ask him if he would succeed in his battle with the Pelishtim.⁷ In response to Shmuel's displeasure at having been

---

3. בראשית ב:ז.

4. תהלים נא:יט.

5. שערי תשובה, שער א' אות כ"א.

6. ברכות יב:.

7. שמואל א פרק כ"ח.

"aroused," Shaul explained that he had no choice but to call upon him, as he hadn't received any guidance from Hashem or the *nevi'im*. He omitted that the *Urim V'Tumim* hadn't helped him either. The reason for this omission, *Chazal* tell us, is that he was embarrassed to mention it, since the reason the *Urim V'Tumim* had not answered him was that he had wiped out Nov, the city of the Kohanim, in retribution for assisting Dovid. Shaul's humiliation was accepted, and it brought him a *kapparah*.

On Yom Kippur, we say the thirteen *Middos HaRachamim* many times. The *Gemara* learns from the *passuk*, "ויעבר ה' על פניו ויקרא," "Hashem passed before him, and He called," that, homiletically speaking, "שנתעטף הקדוש ברוך הוא כשליח צבור והראה לו למשה סדר תפלה, אמר לו, כל זמן שישראל חוטאין יעשו לפני כסדר הזה ואני מוחל להם," "Hashem wrapped Himself in a *tallis*, like a *chazan*, and showed Moshe the procedure of the *tefillah*. He told him, 'Any time *Klal Yisrael* sins, they should do this procedure before me, and I will forgive them.'"[8] What is the significance of Hashem "wrapping Himself" in a *tallis*? It teaches us an essential part of *teshuvah*. The *passuk* in *Tehillim* says, "תפילה לעני כי יעטף," "A prayer of the poor person as he wraps himself."[9] Here, עטיפה is used to refer to a poor person who, so ashamed of his poverty, "wraps" himself to hide. When we beg Hashem for forgiveness, we must similarly hide ourselves in shame, recognizing that we are essentially empty-handed.

As we say in the *Selichos*, "ולנו בושת הפנים," "The shame is ours." If a child or student who misbehaves feels guilty about it, if he is embarrassed, we are more likely to forgive him. On the other hand, if he tries to justify himself, it makes us more upset. Similarly, *Chazal* are teaching us, when Hashem sees that we "hide ourselves" out of shame, we merit forgiveness.

---

8. ראש השנה יז:

9. תהלים קב:א

The Rambam writes in the beginning of *Hilchos Teshuvah*: "כיצד מתודין, אומר, אנא השם, חטאתי עויתי פשעתי לפניך ועשיתי כך וכך, והרי נחמתי ובושתי במעשי, ולעולם איני חוזר לדבר זה," "How does one confess? He says, 'Please, Hashem, I have sinned before you. I did such-and-such, and I feel bad and I am embarrassed from my actions, and I will never go back to this matter.'"[10] First come regret and embarrassment; this is followed by accepting to do better in the future.

When we say in *Viduy*, "על חטא שחטאנו לפניך," "For the sin that we have sinned before You," there are two things we should feel embarrassed about.

The first is our failure to repay Hashem for all His kindnesses. Imagine a person who sees a homeless man sitting on the street and, feeling sorry for him, rents him an apartment. He then gives him a job, helps pay his bills, and marries him off. Eventually, he pays his children's tuition. One day, he tells the man, "You're working very hard. I want to give you a gift." He pays for him and his family to spend Sukkos in Eretz Yisrael. "While you're there," he tells the man, "please visit my father and send him my best regards." When the man returns from his trip, he realizes that he forgot to visit his benefactor's father. He's too embarrassed to face him. After all he had done for him, the man asked of him one little favor, and he didn't do it! The *Ribono Shel Olam* does much more for us. Every breath we take is from Him, as is every step we walk. Everything we have is from Hashem! Should we not feel ashamed when we don't fulfill what He has requested of us?

Rabbi Moshe Cordovero writes at the beginning of *sefer Tomer Devorah* that every time we do a *cheit*, we are essentially using abilities and gifts that Hashem granted us **against** Him.[11] Indeed, this is a large component of *Tefillas Zakah* that is said on Erev Yom Kippur.

Another source of embarrassment when saying *al cheit* is that

---

10. הלכות תשובה א:א

11. תומר דברוה, פרק א׳ מדה א׳

Embarrassed from Cheit 179

when we recognize the greatness of Hashem, it should make us wonder how we could have stooped so low as to sin against Him.

When I was learning in the Gateshead Yeshivah, I went home to London for Shabbos one week in the middle of the winter. That Shabbos, a terrible tragedy took place in our neighborhood. A young woman with ten children, the youngest of them only nine months old, passed away. My friend was the oldest. Being that Gateshead is 300 miles from London, I was the only *bachur* from the Yeshivah present at the *levayah*. Afterwards, I went straight to the *shivah*. Everyone in the house was very shaken, and I decided to do something foolish. I had seen a short article in the local newspaper that weekend about a Rabbi who was caught shoplifting two ties and a belt form Marks and Spencer. I was shocked to read this, as this "Rabbi" was actually a famous Rosh Yeshivah who had just spoken to the whole *Beis Midrash* in Gateshead. Obviously, what most likely had taken place was that his mind was elsewhere at the time, and he didn't even realize that he hadn't paid. I brought the article with me to the *shivah* and showed it to my friend, in attempt to distract him from the tragedy. Over the following days, many cars of *bachurim* came from Gateshead to the *shivah*, and my friend shared the article with all of them. Within two days, the whole Yeshivah was talking about it. I felt terrible. If not for me, nobody would have known about it!

A few years later, I was learning in Eretz Yisrael, and I decided that I wanted to ask *mechilah* from this Rosh Yeshivah. In the end, I was too embarrassed to go over to him. Years later, after I had already moved to Monsey, I saw a sign that this Rosh Yeshivah would be speaking in Yeshivas Bais Shraga. I was still too embarrassed to face him, so I sent my *chavrusa*, Reb Dovid Frankel, to ask for *mechilah* on my behalf. As soon as the Rosh Yeshivah finished the *drashah*, Reb Dovid went over to him and told him that he had a friend who would like to ask for *mechilah*. "I'm *moichel*!" the Rosh Yeshivah said immediately, without waiting to hear what the *mechilah* was for. "If the Rosh Yeshivah knew what my friend did," Reb Dovid said, "the

Rosh Yeshivah might not be *moichel*." "I'm *moichel*, whatever it is!" the Rosh Yeshiva responded. Reb Dovid tried once more. The Rosh Yeshivah got upset and shouted, "I don't care what anyone ever does to me or says about me. I am *moichel b'lev shalem*!" When I heard that, I felt relieved.

If I felt so much embarrassment to stand before a *basar v'dam*, a human being, surely, when we stand in front of Hashem, the *Melech Malchei HaMelachim*, how much more embarrassed we should feel!

On Yom Kippur, we say *Viduy* ten times. Each *Viduy* includes forty-four confessions of "*Al Cheit*," nine confessions of "*Al Chata'im*," and twenty-six confessions in "*Ashamnu*." Let's try to feel true remorse and embarrassment for our misdeeds, and then, as *Chazal* tell us, we will be forgiven for "all our *aveiros*."

AUTHORS BIOGRAPHY

Rabbi Menachem Apter was born and raised in London, England. He learned for many years at the renowned Gateshead Yeshiva in England. From there he continued his Torah learning in the Mir Kollel, Yerushalayim and later, Bais Medrash Elyon in Monsey, New York. Rabbi Apter has been involved in Chinuch for over forty years, teaching various grades and levels. He is currently a Rebbe in Yeshivas Ohr Reuven in Monsey. In addition, Rabbi Apter lectures extensively in shuls, seminaries, summer camps and hotels in North America and Europe on hashkafa topics of personal growth in areas such as gratitude, communication and self-esteem. His lectures are enlightening and overflowing with stories and anecdotes that inspire and delight his listeners.

www.ingramcontent.com/pod-product-compliance
Lightning Source LLC
Chambersburg PA
CBHW050726010526
44107CB00009B/758